What people are saying about

Pagan Portals - Artio and Artaois

Andrew Anderson leads us on a pilgrimage into the wild forests of our Ancestors in search of the ancient Bear Gods of the Celts. Through his own perceptive personal experiences with these little known but intriguing deities, we discover that far from being lost in obscurity, they wait to be rediscovered, still holding a deep relevance and meaning for us today. With some fascinating historical and cultural references, plus useful modern resources and tips for ceremony, this fabulous little book is a wonderful introduction and guide to working with Artio and Artaois.
Philip Carr-Gomm, author of *Druid Mysteries*

This is a beautiful, thoughtful bc   ˆ who loves bears and is curious about Bear God   ent example of how to blend research, hist   ˌonal experience and the insights of other   ˌnly recommended.
Nimue Brown, autho˖   ˌncestors

Pagan Portals: Artio anˑ   ˑrney Towards the Celtic Bear Gods by Andrew Andersoˑ   ˌutifully warm and clear guide to a beloved yet lesser knowˑ pair of Celtic bear divinities. Well researched and deeply personal, this is an excellent, friendly and far reaching guide on a subject that really needs more exploration...*Pagan Portals: Artio and Artaois* is a gift to all those upon the Celtic paths.
Danu Forest, Celtic Scholar and traditional wisewoman, author of several books including *Gwyn ap Nudd* and *The Druid Shaman*

If you're looking for some divine exploration that's a little off the beaten path, look no further than Andrew Anderson's book *Pagan Portals - Artio and Artaois; A Journey Towards the Celtic Bear*

Gods. Though it's short, this book is packed with archaeology, history, comparative mythology, and personal experience that acquaint the reader with the Celtic bear-goddess Artio and her son Artaois. Tying together threads of culture and religion from the Stone Age to the present day, Anderson skillfully connects clues from across Eurasia to flesh out the mythos and meaning of this divine pair. Whether you want to veer off on a new path or simply add another facet to your current spiritual practice, you'll find this book to be a fascinating resource to turn to again and again.

Laura Perry, author of *Ariadne's Thread: Awakening the Wonders of the Ancient Minoans in Our Modern Lives*

A beautiful personal journey of exploration and discovery. You won't fail to fall in love with the spirit of bear once you have read this book.

Rachel Patterson, author of *Pagan Portals - The Cailleach, Arc of the Goddess* and the *Kitchen Witchcraft* series

Pagan Portals - Artio and Artaois is a superb exploration of bears in myth, legend and the natural world. It looks at ancient traditions and representations of bears in the modern world, including films, fiction and art. It is full of wonderful tales, inspiring interviews, and oodles of information. There's information about bear festivals, and insights into the wider cultural significance of bears, such as the gay bear scene. The final chapter suggests practical ways to honour the goddess Artio and the god Artaois, including bear feasts. This is a book to curl up and enjoy in winter hibernation, as well as to learn from throughout the Bear Wheel of the Year.

Lucya Starza, author of *Pagan Portals – Candle Magic, Pagan Portals – Poppets* and *Magical Dolls, Pagan Portals–Guided Visualisations* and A Bad Witch Blog

This book elucidates a little-known and largely forgotten subject - exploring the ancient European links with the bear and also how it connects with Arthurian myth. Well worth reading if you are interested in bears, ancient religion or Celtic culture.

Luke Eastwood, author of *The Druid's Primer* and *The Journey*

Previous Titles by this Author

The Ritual of Writing
ISBN 978 1 78904 153 8

Pagan Portals

Artio and Artaois

A Journey Towards the Celtic Bear Gods

Pagan Portals
Artio and Artaois

A Journey Towards the Celtic Bear Gods

Andrew Anderson

MOON
BOOKS

Winchester, UK
Washington, USA

JOHN HUNT PUBLISHING

First published by Moon Books, 2021
Moon Books is an imprint of John Hunt Publishing Ltd., No. 3 East Street, Alresford
Hampshire SO24 9EE, UK
office@jhpbooks.net
www.johnhuntpublishing.com
www.moon-books.net

For distributor details and how to order please visit the 'Ordering' section on our website.

Text copyright: Andrew Anderson 2020

ISBN: 978 1 78904 462 1
978 1 78904 463 8 (ebook)
Library of Congress Control Number: 2020938309

A CIP catalogue record for this book is available from the British Library.

Design: Stuart Davies

UK: Printed and bound by CPI Group (UK) Ltd, Croydon, CR0 4YY
Printed in North America by CPI GPS partners

We operate a distinctive and ethical publishing philosophy in
all areas of our business, from our global network of authors to
production and worldwide distribution.

Contents

For Mum and Dad

Acknowledgements

Thank you to everyone who discussed their work and worship of bears with me and whose words you will find within this book: Corwen Broch, Kate Fletcher, Ricky Gellissen, Louisa Potter, Beth Wildwood and Hannah Willow.

Thank you again to Beth Wildwood for the stunning artwork on the cover, which was designed specifically for this book.

Thank you to Sue Knott for her beautiful illustrations of the Artio and Gallos statues.

Thank you to Guenter Nal and Eva Funk for a fantastic tour of Bern, discussing the city, bears and all things Druidic! And an enormous thank you to Eva for helping with translations of key information from the Bern Historical Museum. Thank you also to Lesley and Dereck for helping with the journey.

Thanks to Sandi and Dave for letting me stay at their home in North Carolina, and to Wendy and Bernie for taking me and looking after me! Happy days, never forgotten.

Many thanks to the excellent staff and volunteers at Bear Wood in The Wild Place Project for all their help and advice during my visit.

Thank you to Trevor and Nimue for the ongoing help and support.

Thank you also to Valentina Bernardi, Bee Helygen and Daniel McKenzie.

To Marlowe (my Little Bear) and Alfie for being there.

And for Becky, for everything.

Introduction

The Edges of the Forest

I first encountered Artio on a very turbulent evening. I had seen her name before on a friend's Facebook feed when they had shared a meme where a particularly evangelical bear appeared through a door, asking "Excuse me, do you have a moment to talk about the Goddess Artio?" However, that had been the extent of my experience until she decided to visit me.

It was a dark, wintry evening and I was spending the last night in my own bed. I was going away to Glastonbury the next day and I was incredibly worried about leaving my loved ones, my cats and my home. I'd spent most of my time lying awake worrying about leaving, thinking about what would happen if the house was broken into or vandalised, so I decided I'd call on higher powers to help me. I asked, very generally, for a God or Goddess to help me, to protect my home while I was away.

Suddenly, I had a vision of an enormous translucent She-Bear standing head and shoulders above my home, roaring deeply and protectively. She roared and roared again, warding off any ill that dare settle on my doorstep. The roars resonated through my being and I knew that my home would be safe while I was away. I also instinctively knew the name of my new found guardian: I had met the Goddess Artio.

Assuming that she was a fairly major figure in the Celtic pantheon, I began to research her and found, to my amazement, that there was very little archaeological or written information about her. I felt that, if she was calling to me, I should discover more about her. I decided to make my exploration a pilgrimage, both physically and spiritually, towards understanding Artio. Along the way, I found she had a male counterpart called Artaois, or Artaius. I began making assumptions about his character

1

from wider cultural attitudes but, as I got closer to him, I found that they were not always accurate. I decided to include him in my pilgrimage to see if I could find out who he was beneath the layers of inference.

This book is about my journey towards the Celtic Bear Gods. My first book for Moon Books was *The Ritual of Writing*, which encouraged the reader to use writing as part of their spiritual practice. This book takes that idea one step further; it is a piece of devotional writing about my experiences with Artio and Artaois as I seek to deepen my relationship with them.

While you are reading this book, I would ask you reflect on Miranda Green's statement that

"The evidence of archaeology is at best incomplete and ambiguous; at worst, it is misleading and confusing. The survival (or lack of it) of the evidence is one problem; its interpretation is another ... any attempt at an explanation of Celtic religion must at best be extremely speculative - a construction, rather than a reconstruction."[1].

Please bear in mind that this is my own personal journey towards Artio and Artaois; you may have a different interpretation, a different sense of who they are. However, I hope you find something here which will enlighten your path towards them.

Chapter 1

Paw Prints across Europe

Finding Artio

Bear worship, also known as Arctolatry, is a form of spiritual observance which can be found in many ancient cultures around the world, particularly those in the northern hemisphere. Evidence for such beliefs in central Europe can be found in a collection of "stone altars and significant caches of bear bones at Drachenloch in Switzerland [which] shows us that Neanderthal man revered the cave bear as Master of Animals as far back as 70,000 years ago."[1] While it is unclear whether or not bear worship was a constant feature in this region across the centuries, during the Romano-Celtic period we find two deities in the same region named Artio and Artaois. Both of their names stem from the Celtic root word Artos[2] which means 'Bear' and both have survived to a greater or lesser extent for us today. As I had a greater connection to Artio, I decided to begin my investigations with her.

In terms of the historical record, surprisingly little evidence exists for a Celtic Goddess named Artio, and that which does can be confusing to follow. It feels at times like tracking pawprints through a forest. In this case, however, the pawprints are sparse. Miranda Green notes that "Bears are very rare in the archaeological record"[3] from this period. If bears themselves are rare, then it should, perhaps, be no surprise that a bear deity may not be represented in abundance. However, the fact that there is more than one piece of evidence for Artio shows that she was of some importance as "the epigraphic record of the Romano-Celtic period reveals about 400 god-names, over 300 of which occur only once"[4]. Artio, at least, was deemed to be significant enough to appear in several inscriptions and artefacts across central and western Europe, which we are lucky enough to still possess.

As my intention was to frame my discovery of Artio as a journey or a pilgrimage towards understanding, I decided to create a map showing a path of the physical, historical evidence stretching across Europe, to get a sense of where she had been in the past and how I could find my way to her. What follows is a list of the material artefacts that provide evidence for the worship of Artio. The first piece of evidence I found about Artio seemed to be in the small town of Weilerbach in Luxemburg.[5] Here there appeared to be an inscription which reads "ARRTIONI BIBER", which broadly translates as an offering to Artio from a devotee named Biber. Upon cross-referencing this information, I found that Green places the inscription in a similar area, although just over the German border, noting that "[Artio] was worshipped in the remote Bollendorf Valley, her name inscribed on the rocky sides of the defile".[6] This in turn led me to discover that the inscription is in a valley, now a tourist attraction, called Schweineställe in the municipality of Ernzen.[7]

These small geographical differences felt quite confusing as I was craving conclusive and definitive answers. Here, at the beginning, as would be the case for the whole journey, I found that certainty was somewhat elusive and that I would need to work hard to try and pin down the trail of Artio.

Approximately 70 kilometres east of the inscription is the German town of Daun, where another inscription can be found. This one reads "ARTIO AGRITIVS", a similar dedication to that above but this time from Agritus.[8] Around this time, I found a reference by author Marija Gimbutas[9] to several Artio inscriptions in Bitburg. Further work has led me to believe that this is a conflation of the two inscriptions in Daun and Ernzen, with Bitburg standing somewhere in between them in the Rhinish Palatinate.

Further east into Germany there is a third inscription to Artio at Heddernheim, near Frankfurt, which simply reads "[DEAE

AR]TIONI" [10] To the south east of Frankfurt is the community Stockstadt am Main, where there is a more complex inscription which reads: "[DEAE A]RTIONI SACR(VM)] .[...]S SEXTI(VS) S[...] [...D]E SV[O POS(VIT)]".[11] This dedication is "To the Sacred goddess Artio" from the Roman citizen with a standard three part name (or Tria Nomina) with only his middle name, Sextus, remaining complete.[12]

There are some references to other pieces of physical evidence which relate to Artio which have proved more difficult to track down. One example is a reference to inscriptions in Huerta and Sigüenza in Spain.[13] Currently I have been unable to find any further information about what these could be.

So, after collating all of the physical evidence from the inscriptions, the trail of evidence for Artio runs in an almost straight line from the Luxemburg border in the west approximately 250 kilometres east to Stockstadt am Main. And then it takes a sharp turn 450 kilometres south.

By far the most compelling piece of material evidence for Artio is a bronze statue found at Muri in Switzerland, now housed in the Bern Historical Museum. There are pictures of the statue on-line but I felt that, if I was serious about undertaking a spiritual journey towards Artio then I needed to make a physical pilgrimage to see the statue in Bern. I wanted to see the statue with my own eyes, to get a sense of its contours and construction and to see if I could find something new about her.

The name of the Swiss city Bern comes from the word "Bear". The city was established in 1191 by Berthold V, Duke of Zähringen who decreed that the first animal killed in the vicinity would give its name to the city. As such, when a bear was hunted and killed, the city took on its name and a bear appears on the city's coat of arms.

I decided that I was going to take a train to Bern, rather than fly. I felt it was far more environmentally friendly to travel by train rather than by plane and, as this was the beginning of a spiritual journey, I felt it was important to honour the earth (or at least do as little harm as possible) on my journey. Similarly, the sense that I was on a pilgrimage was incredibly important to me. I wanted the experience of seeing the landscape change around me as I travelled towards my destination. And so, I booked train tickets for a post-Lughnasadh pilgrimage to Bern.

My journey took me first to London, where I took the Eurostar under the English Channel to Paris. From there, I began my journey eastwards. The golden, rolling agricultural fields of central France slowly began to make way for different terrain after we passed through Dijon. The hills seemed to be a bit steeper and I could feel the high-speed train strain a little more as the inclines got that bit more challenging. More pine trees began to appear in the forest groves and the whole place felt a little wilder. Bears seemed a more likely discovery in this deeper, greener region. Just before the town of Mulhouse, the mountains came into view.

It was around this point in my journey that I started to get a little nervous. I was far beyond any city I had visited; I was on my own and a voice inside me was suggesting that I should have stayed at home. Arriving at the station in the Swiss city of Basel, I just missed my connection to the capital. I decided to have a look around some shops on the concourse. I wandered up and down but nothing really took my fancy. I stopped next to the window of a large stationery store. I looked into the window and, staring out at me were two cartoon bears in an embrace. It was a greetings card with the phrase "I love you. Big bear hugs" emblazoned across it! You may think that is coincidence, but after my self-doubt on the train, there was a sense that Artio was reaching out and welcoming me as I approached the final stage of my journey.

As my train headed out of Basel, I found myself in what I thought was the heart of the wooded mountains. In the next few days, I would see the Eiger and the Jungfrau from the Parliament

Plaza in Bern and realise that I had actually been passing through hills rather than mountains, but for a lowland Englander like myself, the landscape felt magically mountainous! The train began to spend longer and longer underground as it charged through tunnels carved into the hills. This gave a deeply grounded sensation to the final stage of the journey, so deep that, at times, it made me close my eyes as I felt quite dizzy.

Bern is a magical place. The centre of the city is a UNESCO world heritage site, so retains much of its medieval architecture. After settling into my hotel, which overlooked the turquoise river Aare, I began to explore the central streets of the old town, Gerchtigkeitsgasse and Kramgasse. It felt like a completely different world, a place where characters from myths and fairy tales could come barrelling around the corner. I decided to find some food and try to connect to the spirit of place, so I found one of the quieter eateries and set myself up overlooking the old town. Once settled, I began to ask if Artio was present and the answer was immediate. The same figure who had appeared to me when I had asked for protection on that dark night at home appeared again but far more powerfully. She was absolutely enormous, towering, head and shoulders over the streets of the city so that I had to look up, over the roofs of Gerchtigkeitsgasse to see her. There was a rainbow quality to her pelt and she was resplendent in a regal headband.

Knowing I was in the right place for the next stage of my discoveries, I headed back to my hotel for an early night.

One of the reasons I had picked my hotel was because of its proximity to Bern's biggest attraction; the Bärengraben or Bear Garden. Also known as the Bärenpark, this area houses three beautiful brown bears called Finn, Björk and Ursina in the heart of the city. Bern has a long history of keeping bears with the first bear pit being established in 1513, when a young bear was captured in a military campaign. Although the idea of bear pits may seem cruel to us now, there is no doubt how important bears have been to the Bernese throughout their history. I found an interesting piece of information at the site referring to an invasion and occupation by the French in 1798, where the removal of the bears to Paris was framed as an 'abduction'. Visiting the Bärengraben today, the bear pit built in 1857 is still in use and seems incredibly small to modern sensibilities. The other, smaller pit which stands nearby, built in 1924 to house the young bears, is now a bistro and exhibition about the history of the site. It is interesting to walk around in this space and get a sense of the confinement those bears would have experienced.

When I arrived at the at the Bärengraben for my first visit, Finn, Björk, and Ursina were confined in the 1857 pit. Finn did not seem happy and was pacing around the space, digging at one of the doors. His mate, Björk, sat on rocks in the middle of the enclosure, while their daughter Ursina sat quietly near her father. As it turned out, this would be the only time I would see all three of the bears together and in one place. The bears seemed frustrated in the pit, being, as it is, surrounded by people and close to a busy road.

However, it soon became clear that they were only there while their keepers did some essential maintenance on the rest of their home. Although the 1857 pits were improved in the 1990s, calls for a bigger enclosure led to the building of the wider Bärenpark which was opened in 2009 and the site was improved again recently. The bears can now wander through a large garden which runs down steeply to the river Aare. There are plenty of places for the bears to hide under trees and in the undergrowth and they can bathe in deep water which runs along the bottom of the site. This area is connected to the pit by tunnels where there the bears can stay well out of sight of visitors.

While there is a sense of the conquered beast about the bear pit in the main plaza, the wider Bärenpark is an absolute joy to visit. No, it is not ideal that these animals are in captivity, but they are treated in an incredibly respectful way and there seems to be constant reassessment of the site to improve the quality of the bears' lives. For example, pictures of the Bärenpark from 2009 show the site as a grassy hill, with few spaces for the bears to hide. Today, they can hide themselves in an array of dense undergrowth and do their best to ignore the humans, who desperately seek out a glimpse of these beloved creatures. As such, it became a place I returned to again and again throughout my stay, just to be close to the bears, even if I couldn't see them.

The object of my visit, the statue of Artio, is housed in the Bernisches Historisches Museum, a short if steep walk along the Aare from the Bärenpark. From the outside it resembles a fairy tale castle on the corner of a busy road junction. The entrance to the museum is guarded by two giant stone bears who look down sagely at the visitors passing beneath. The museum is excellent and houses an outstanding exhibition on Einstein. However, I was there to see Artio, so as soon as I bought my ticket, I set out to find her.

I discovered her standing in a central case towards the end

Statue of Artio by Sue Knott

of an exhibition on the Celts. The statue itself consists of several pieces. A somewhat plain base which supports the figure of a seated female seemingly being confronted by a large bear. There is also a tree behind the bear and an elevated bowl of fruit next to the woman. It is displayed with several other bronze statues, including those of Minerva, Juno and Jupiter, which were found during the excavations at Muri. The Artio piece stands in front of them and is the focus of the display, although, surprisingly, she seems to get little attention. As I later discovered, there is not even a postcard of the statue in the shop.

I was a bit worried about making a fool of myself when I first saw the statue, after all I had travelled a long way on a spiritual pilgrimage to see it and I thought it would be an emotional moment. I did not want other people to see me burst into tears in the middle of the museum, so I braced myself before I walked into the room. It was a pretty pointless thing to do because, as soon as I saw the statue in the case, a wave of joy came over me and I did indeed begin to cry, overwhelmed at the sight of the ancient icon I was approaching. However, there was no one else in the exhibit. In total, I spent nearly an hour with the statue and during that time only three other people came in: a man came through quickly, taking photos of all of the exhibits except for the statue of Artio, and two young women came in, looked around quickly and left. Apart from that, I was alone with the statue. At one point the lights in the exhibition switched off because I was so still and no one else had been in for so long!

There is an energy that comes from the statue when you see it in real life, rather than in books or online. That power could come from the original intention of this statue, hinted at on the base which is inscribed with the phrase "DEAE ARTONI LICINIA SABINILLA" or dedicated to "the goddess Artio (by) Licinia Sabinilla".[14] As a devotional figure, possibly for use in a temple or private altar, Green suggests that originally "the god would be considered as dwelling within that image"[15]. As such, there was a sense that by arriving at the statue I had arrived at the closest point to Artio that I had ever been and could ever get. That energy, that excitement, filled my time with her.

Face to face with the statue, it began to reveal its secrets. The piece is far more beautiful than I had realised, but also more fragile. The plinth on which the figures stand is damaged and there is a hole beneath the bear's feet. However, the biggest revelation came from information next to the statue. Up until that point, all of the information I had found about the Artio statue had suggested that she was the human female figure in the arrangement. Green states that the piece is "an image of the goddess and her bear"[16] while J.M.C. Toynbee states "Artio had a tame bear, delightfully portrayed in bronze"[17]. However, the information in the exhibition clearly states that "The Celtic Bear Goddess Artio is depicted as a powerful She-bear and at the same time as a human figure".

While the idea that Artio is both the human and the bear is widely accepted, it was only by visiting the museum I discovered that only one of the figures originally stood on the plinth, as evidenced by welding marks on the base. "Originally the bear stood alone on the pedestal ... At a later date the tree was moved to the semi-circular projection behind the bear to make room for the enthroned goddess"[18] Although it was likely that the inscription was added at the same time as the human figure, there is a clear sense here that it was the figure of the bear, not the human, which originally represented the embodiment of Artio.

I think it is interesting to note at this point that, whenever I have met Artio, she has always appeared as a bear rather than in a human form. I wondered if that would change as I approached her homeland but she has always remained resolutely in bear form, something that resonated even more strongly with me after I made these discoveries about the statue.

The bear is such a dominant part of the statue that it is the first piece which draws the eye. She is incredibly beautiful. Her fur is delineated in lines which, in places, look like stars. The bear's face is charming and reminded me of Finn's face from the bear pit that morning, as he looked up at me. He had looked me straight in the face and blinked repeatedly, a trait which I recognized from my cats and which I call "friendly eyes". The bear on the plinth has the same face, her eyes look almost sleepy, as if she is giving "friendly eyes" both to the human in front of her and those looking at her. While her mouth is open and her teeth bared, again, it does not feel aggressive. Her tongue lolls out, possibly as if she were hungry or hot. She may initially look like she is squaring up to the human figure in front of her, her stance being very dominant, but it rather feels like she is inviting you in to stroke and fuss her, not that she is being in any sense confrontational.

Annemarie Kaufmann-Heinimann notes that the human figure on the plinth, sitting on a now missing throne, is of a "Vegetationsgöttin"[19] or vegetation goddess. The figure is certainly linked to ideas of the harvest as she appears to have emptied a bowl of fruit and corn over herself, as if she were submitting to the bear and encouraging it to eat from her lap. Kaufmann-Heinimann proposes that this statue once stood separately as a more generic vegetation goddess before being unified with the bear on the plinth to become Artio. Green seemingly expands the figure's role beyond that of simply a vegetation goddess by noting that "Images of a goddess associated with life and abundance are physical manifestations of a community endeavouring to control the behaviour of the seasons and to appease and propitiate the forces who imposed the cycle of life and death".[20] In their seminal book on bear lore *The Sacred Paw*, Paul Shepherd and Barry Sanders suggest that, for many cultures, bears were a potent symbol of rebirth, with female bears emerging after a period of hibernation or 'denning' deep in the earth, not only alive, but with young: "Clearly the bear was a master of renewal and the wheel of the seasons, of the knowledge of when to die and when to be reborn".[21] Perhaps it was this sense of potency and renewal which led to Licinia Sabinilla placing the vegetation goddess next to the statue of the bear and using it as a devotional piece.

While it is tempting to look simply at the bear or the human figure to identify the characteristics of Artio, I personally feel we have to look at the piece as a whole. This is an idea not pursued by any of the authors I have previously read, but thinking of the statue in this way reveals a new interpretation. Artio's meaning lies not in one single piece but in every element, in the friendly bear, the generous Goddess and her basketful of fruit. For me, meaning also resides in the tree which stands behind the bear. The tree is very stylised, not identifiable as any particular genus of tree and seems to have a somewhat phallic acorn pointing over the bear's back. Many writers dismiss the tree simply as "representative of the wild forest [the bear] inhabits".[22] However, I feel it needs a little more consideration as there are strong connections between the bear and the tree as symbols of rebirth:

> In the bear the tree has a metaphysical symbiotic partner, a companion in the art of immortality. The bear, like the tree, seems to die but, in the spring, is discovered not to have died. And so it is said that, even when killed it does not truly die. Like the tree, with its roots, trunk, and limbs in different layers of the cosmos, the bear is seen in the stars in the night sky, underground as the sleeper and on earth as an animal. [23]

Meaning that, taken together, the bear, the human, the fruit and the tree present a powerful image of rebirth and of plenty, a dedication to an extremely powerful protective mother.

It was difficult to leave the museum after such an intense time working with the statue. But Bern is full of bear energy so it felt like the Goddess was all around me. There are bears everywhere around the city: bear statues, bear paintings, bear souvenirs. I even got a lift to the station in a Bärentaxi! And yet, something felt slightly amiss to me. I began to wonder how much of Bern's enthusiasm for bears came from Artio and how much came from the decree by Berthold V, so I began asking local people I met. The answer was pretty clear. Few of them had ever heard of Artio. I was stunned! The city of bears is home to the most beautiful devotional piece of bronze made to honour a Bear Goddess and no one knew about it! Of course, this matched up with my experience in the museum, where I was mostly alone and where the visitors failed to take notice of the statue of Artio. I met up with some friends and fellow Druids on my last day and asked them directly about the connection between the city and Artio. They confirmed that she was not particularly well known. Through our discussions, however, we did note the interesting appearance of bear energy in the area during the Neolithic, then again during the Celtic period, when it was a centre for a bear cult, which was augmented with a more human face by the Romans and which, although it disappeared (or hibernated) for many years, re-established itself from the 1100s in a city which embraced the bear as its symbol and its name. Although there isn't a direct, unbroken like back to Artio in Bern, it still felt very much, to me, like her city.

I spent my last evening in Bern back at the Bärengraben, watching Finn lumber up and down the steps of his enclosure and taking a dip in the water, much to the delight of everyone by the Aare. The bears in the Bärengraben give Bern its heart. People love visiting the site and they genuinely love seeing the bears. Bern has an energy which is deep and abiding. It is welcoming, nurturing, and peaceful. It is Artio's energy. I really did not want to leave.

Tracking Artaois

I first heard of Artaois in Philip and Stephanie Carr-Gomm's divination set *The Druid Animal Oracle*. Here, drawing the card of the bear means "you are connected ... to the Bear God Artaois"[24]. But who was Artaois? Well, if physical the evidence for Artio is slim, then evidence for Artaois is even more difficult to find and rests on a single inscription. Green states that "the divine patron of bears ... Mercury Artaios was venerated at Beaucroissant (Isère)."[25] Beaucroissant is a town in south eastern France, close to Lyon and about 300 kilometers south west of Bern. The inscription there reads "MERCVRIO AVG(USTO) ARTAIO SACR(VM) SEX(TVS) GEMINVS CVPITVS EX VOTO"[26] or "To the august Mercury Artaius, Sextus Geminius Cupitus (has dedicated this) sacred (stone) in fulfillment of a vow"[27]. As you can see, there are variations in the spelling of Artaois' name here, although this is clearly the God to whom the Carr-Gomms are referring to.

Having only one inscription to Artaois should not necessarily come as a surprise: do not forget there are over 300 Celtic Gods who only appear once in the historical record.[28] The fact that his name is used as an epithet, or a description of another thing, may seem strange but was a fairly common practice when the Romans arrived in Celtic lands. Green writes:

> The shadowy, multi-functional and more localised gods of the Celts and the more formal Roman pantheon produced a hybrid religious culture ... it appears that the Romans naively assumed that Celtic gods were Roman ones.[29]

In other words, the inscription shows that the Romans assumed that Artaois was an incarnation of Mercury, or at least shared traits with him. Marie-Louise Sjoestedt takes this one stage further, noting that "a single Roman deity represents a multiplicity of local gods whose memory is preserved in the epithet of the imported foreigner".[30] In fact, 19 different Celtic gods are remembered as epithets to Mercury, while 59 are remembered as epithets to Mars.[31]

What does this association with Mercury tell us about Artaois? Well, it could give us a hint as to some of his qualities. Caesar wrote "Among the gods [the Celts] most worship Mercury. There are numerous images of him; they declare him the inventor of all arts, the guide for every road and journey, and they deem him to have the greatest influence for all money-making and traffic".[32] While some care has to be used with this view (after all, Caesar was an invader and not a Celt, and the epithet data shows that more attention was paid to Mars than Mercury) it is still an interesting insight into Artaois' possible qualities. Praying to a Bear God for help during journeys, particularly those through forested areas, would make sense. A possible role in "money-making" could be seen to parallel Artio's role as a goddess of plenty, as could the sense of him being "the inventor of all arts", bringing ideas to fruition.

However, what is noticeably lacking here is the sense of Artaois as a warrior. This is surprising considering that "The greatest compliment that could be paid to a hero in the Celtic tradition was to describe him as *Art an neart* – a bear in vigour".[33] While Mercury's role seems to be that of nurturer and protector, the role of warrior fits more with the Roman god of war, Mars. So, by aligning Artaois with Mercury instead, are we to infer that Artaois did not have warrior qualities? Sjoestedt believes not, stating that tribal gods such as Artaois "must have been regarded sometimes as a god of war and sometimes as a god of industry, according as he was invoked in times of war or peace".[34] That does seem to make sense. Those honouring a Bear God surely wouldn't turn away from him in times of conflict when a bear's physical strength and protective nature would be a benefit.

So, while Artaois' association with Mercury is helpful in ascribing him some roles, it is important not to limit him to those which just seem to apply to Mercury. In fact, before being subsumed by his association with Mercury, Artaois was a tribal or chief god "father, nurturer, protector of the tribe, warrior, magician and craftsman, the Teutates of universal activity and total efficiency".[35]

Having considered the archaeological evidence and explored the city of Bern, I decided to expand my understanding of Artio and Artaois in a more creative way. I was drawn to the work of Beth Wildwood, who I discovered on Instagram (@beth_wildwood) and Facebook (Wild Spirit Weaver). As an artist, Beth works with a range of animal images, including bears, and creates her work on natural materials found near her home in the Rothaar Mountains of Germany, about 600 kilometres north of Bern. I first discovered Beth's work a few years ago when I bought an Equinox Bear from her for my altar. The small wooden statue of a bear is painted on both sides and is meant to be turned around at the Spring and Autumn Equinoxes. During the light half of the year the statue faces to the right. A beautiful European brown bear is revealed, highlighted in gold with an abstracted sunshine on its haunches. For the dark half of the year, the bear faces to the left. This time it is presented as a black bear with silver stars and a pale blue moon adorning its coat. This figure has become an integral part of my altar since it arrived from Germany, so I decided to contact Beth and ask her about her work with bears.

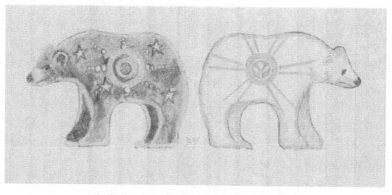

Solstice Bears by Beth Wildwood

I started by asking her about her inspiration for creating the Equinox Bears. "They came in to being through dreamwork at a time when I needed to find balance, clarity and stillness in my life" she told me. "So, they represent balance and are dual in nature; both the sun and the moon, light and darkness". However, her work with this aspect bears is clearly still on-going. "They have become very close and at every Equinox I give life to a few more figures for others to use. I like to invite others to open their own portals and work with bear in their own way."

I wondered if the image of the bear was something Beth had always worked with. She told me that she and her family had travelled much when she was younger and that she had settled in the Rothaar mountains in 2006. "It wasn't until I came to Germany, here in the wildwood, that the land and nature really opened to me. Even though I painted the bear when I lived elsewhere, the deeper connection was not there. I was drawn to working with other animals so I guess I wasn't ready for the amazing bear spirit that I have come to know here in my wild home."

"In recent years I have been greatly drawn to working with the spirit of the bear. I came across some wonderful Finnish folklore, particularly the figure of 'Honey Paw of the Mountains'". Honey Paw was an epithet used for the great bear spirit, who was traditionally worshipped in Finland.[36] "A creative spark led me to create the seven spirit figures of bears as part of my 'Honey Paw Project'. Each figure holds its own magic as a working tool. The seven figures represent the Honey Paw archetype, nurture, protection, the shaman, healing, dreamtime and the guardian." Although Beth's inspiration for these figures comes from Finnish mythology, there are clear links to the attributes I had found in Artio and Artaois. I asked Beth which of the figures was her favourite "My particular favourite is the spirit bear of the dreamtime. It represents the great spirit of the bear as it sleeps in the winter earth. New life is born and we can delve into the infinite source of bear wisdom to dream and evolve."

Finally, I asked Beth whether she knew of Artio and Artaois, and whether they inspire her: "It seems the bear has been very important spiritually for thousands of years and worshipped all over the world. Even though I am aware of the Bear Gods and Goddesses I try not to let this mythology seep into my art but to draw from the divine well of inspiration and let new waves appear."

I find Beth's approach here incredibly interesting; although she is trying to draw inspiration from a deeper source, there are clear echoes of both Artio and Artaois in her work and the different aspects of her seven figures add new dimensions to our consideration of the Celtic bear gods.

After my initial journeys, and even despite limited physical evidence, I was beginning to get a sense of both Artio and Artaois. Artio is an Earth Goddess, a strongly maternal figure, at once welcoming and nurturing but also fiercely protective. Her statue shows her to be a Goddess of abundance, of the harvest in the natural world. Along with that is the sense that she is a Goddess of rebirth and renewal, with "the knowledge of when to die and when to be reborn".[37] Through his associations with Mercury, Artaois also has similar associations with harvests, but this time of trade and commerce. More widely, we can see him as a tribal god "father, nurturer, protector of the tribe, warrior, magician and craftsman".[38] While there may be some similarities between their characteristics, there is also an important distinction to make at this stage: "we have a male principle of society to which is opposed a female principle of nature, or rather ... social forces of male character opposed by natural forces of female character."[39] In other words, Artio is a Goddess of nature while Artaois is a God of humankind. With this definition of their characteristics, I turned my attention to finding Artio and Artaois closer to home.

Chapter 2

Pawprints across Britain.

Tracking Artaois

While I was exploring the European roots for Artio and Artaois, a surprising advert popped up on social media: "Bears are Back"[1] it exclaimed. Well, how could I resist?! Clicking the link, I found an exciting promise: "Thousands of years ago, European brown bears lived right here in Britain. In 2019, Wild Place Project is bringing them back!"[2] Thrilled by the synchronicity of my discovery, I decided this would be the best place to begin my exploration of bears in Britain. So, on a beautiful drizzly Monday in September, I headed to Bristol.

Wild Place Project is a small animal park, part of Bristol Zoo, just off the M5 near the shopping mecca Cribbs Causeway. While it has many features of a traditional zoo, Bear Wood is whole different experience for visitors, and for bears. Arriving at the entrance to the exhibit, I stepped into a small circular room which doubled as a time machine. A short film transports the visitor back through time to the year 8000BC, to a time when Britain was far wilder and was covered in approximately 75% woodland. I emerged onto a wooden walkway in the canopy of a beautiful autumnal Oak wood, full of birdsong.

The spirit of conservation runs deep at Wild Place: "Bear Wood isn't just about what we've lost. It is also about fighting to protect what we have. Today only 2% of Britain's ancient woodland has survived being cut down, and offers a vital habitat for threatened species such as greater-spotted woodpeckers, tawny owls and hedgehogs".[3] Rather than only focusing on their furry inhabitants, the exhibit also gives visitors a lot of information about the ecology of forests and individual trees. It really is a beautiful experience and gives a totally different perspective on our native woodlands.

Despite the sound of children, the background roar of the M5 and a slightly incongruous view of the Prince of Wales bridge across the Severn, I really did feel as if I was deep in the forest. The experience felt really primal and elemental, as if I was back in the ancestral past. The fact that visitors look down from the walkway above means that they are largely ignored by those who live on the woodland floor. Rather like the Bärengraben, there are no guarantees that you will see any of the animals as they wander around significant sized enclosures. I timed my visit with feeding, so my first encounter was not with a bear but with a surprisingly fierce wolverine, crunching her way through a whole quail. I was also lucky to spot the lynxes, who are very secretive and keep themselves well hidden.

The stars of the show are the bears, four young European brown bears who have the run of most of the site. They are brothers Neo and Nilas, alongside brother and sister Albie and Gemini. They are filled with youthful exuberance and a spirit of adventure, which is lucky because these bears are part of a unique project. While they currently have the run of several enclosures, early in 2020 Wild Place will begin to integrate them with the pack of five wolves who peer inquisitively from the next enclosure: "The fact that the bears and wolves have a 10,000 square metre wooded paddock to share should help. They can keep away from each other if they want and interact if the mood takes them."[4] While some may baulk at this experiment, there is a real sense that the project is genuinely trying to recreate our ancient woodlands where bears and wolves used to mix. Talking to the staff and volunteers, it is clear to see how passionately they believe in this project. There is a sense of expertise and care which permeates their work, with the sense that they are part of something incredibly exciting.

I got my close encounter towards the end of my visit in the bear viewing area, a concrete and glass bunker down on the forest floor. The giant paw and claw marks on the outside of the windows were a startling reminder of just how powerful bears are. As I stood there in awe at the sheer power of these creatures, Gemini wandered up to a nearby tree and began foraging. I was so taken with her and what she was doing that I didn't notice Albie walking along right next to the glass! For a few moments they were right there in front of me, male and female, brother and sister, God and Goddess, back in a British woodland where their ancestors used to roam.

As you move through the exhibit at Wild Place, there are several points where time seemingly jumps forward, leaving you at the end in a woodland in the 21st Century, where our woods are bearless. So, when did bears die out in Britain? The answer to that question is incredibly difficult, if not impossible, to answer. The most recent study on the presence of bears in Britain is by Hannah O'Regan, who states "determining when wild animals were present in the past is not straight-forward, particularly when dealing with an animal such as the brown bear where furs … and live animals … can be moved and traded over considerable distances over long periods."[5] Not surprisingly she suggests that it was human activity which led to bears becoming extinct here: "a combination of climate change and landscape change through human activity [were] the main drivers of bear extinction in Holocene Europe. Habitat fragmentation may have resulted in smaller populations that would have been more vulnerable to extinction."[6] In the end she proposes two somewhat depressing theories as to when bears became extinct in Britain. Firstly "the bear became extinct in the late Neolithic / early Bronze Age and other [archaeological] findings represent imported specimens (dead or alive)"[7] or secondly that "bears remained present but in low, almost undetectable numbers until the early medieval period, before finally becoming extinct".[8] It seems that the vision of the bear filled woodland which Wild Place gave me is a very ancient dream indeed.

Coming back to 21st Century Britain, and particularly the M5, was a horrible shock to the system. As I drove home, I reflected that none of the archaeological evidence that O'Regan considers in her article was connected to my home county, Warwickshire, and yet I am surrounded by bears. I live in Stratford-upon-Avon and the most well-known stage direction by the town's famous son, William Shakespeare, is "Exit, pursued by a bear" from Act 3, scene 3 of *The Winter's Tale*. There is still an interesting debate over whether a real bear or an actor in a bear skin would have been used for this particular stage effect. Phillip Henslowe, a well-known theatre manager of the time, was known to have a bear collection which included "two polar bear cubs [which] were brought back from the waters off Greenland in 1609"[9]. Although it may seem strange to use a real bear in performance, the cubs' age may well have been a factor as "Polar bears become fierce at pubescence and were relegated to bear baiting, but the cubs were apparently still trainable."[10]

Bear baiting, the apparent sport of chaining a bear to a post and letting it be attacked by dogs, was a popular pastime in Shakespeare's day, with pits very close to the Globe Theatre. The activity has a very obvious connection to Warwickshire. The Warwickshire coat of arms depicts a bear muzzled and chained to a large post, or ragged staff as it is more commonly called, as if it were about to be baited. It's interesting to note that the more modern Warwickshire County Council logo simply has the bear leaning on the staff without either the chains or the muzzle. This was changed in the early 1990s "because of animal welfare concerns" and to give a "more modern image for an organisation going through a period of modernisation itself."[11]

I wondered if this coat of arms could help me get any closer to Artaois. It appears that the coat of arms was first used by the Earls of Warwick in 1268 where the bear "implied boldness and courage".[12] Shepherd and Sanders, however, think that Guy of Warwick had another motive to using the bear on the

23

sigil. They note that the bear was "a device adopted by other medieval knights of lesser light in their attempts to stand in [King] Arthur's historic/legendary glow."[13] Indeed, it seems that the Earl of Warwick went so far as to create a legendary ancestor from the same period and with the same root name as Arthur, to seal that connection: "William Dugdale, writing in the 1650s, said that Arthgal, an Earl of Warwick at the time of King Arthur, thought that his name came from the Welsh "artos" or bear."[14]

Sensing a connection between the legendary King Arthur and the description of Artaois as "father, nurturer, protector of the tribe, warrior, magician and craftsman"[15], I wondered if any connections had been made between them. Dan Puplett certainly seems to think so, suggesting that: "The bear god Artaois is closely linked to the warrior-king, Arthur; with his legendary strength and fighting prowess, Arthur's name and emblem both represent this animal."[16] Puplett clearly focusses on Arthur's warrior or chieftain role as the connection between the two. This link between the manifestation of the bear god, Artaois, and a warrior chief, may be echoed in the burial of a "young late Iron age chieftan whose remains were interred in a rich grave at Welwyn (Herts) [after being] laid on a bearskin".[17] A similar cremation was found at Baldock, Hertfordshire, where "Three burned bear phalanges ... [were] mixed with the remains of human cremation."[18] O'Regan notes that this type of burial was rare in this period and that "wild animal remains are missing from sites because there was a deliberate distancing of human society from the natural world [during the Iron Age]. However, many of these animals were still represented in art, while the bear was not. The lack of specimens and iconography suggests that the bear was absent, at least in southern and Eastern England, during the Iron Age."[19] If this is the case, then clothing a chieftain in a difficult to obtain bear skin could hold extra significance, aligning them with a powerful tribal deity or notable warrior.

T. W. Rolleston develops that sense of connection between the Arthur and Artaois much further, suggesting that, when we are considering Arthur, we are actually considering Artaois:

Tales of a British chief named Arthur were probably taken to Brittany by Welsh exiles at about the sixth century. They must also have brought legends of the Celtic deity Artaius, and these two personages ultimately blended into one. An Arthur saga thus arose, and this became a centre around which clustered a mass of floating legendary matter relating to various Celtic figures, both human and divine.[20]

Rolleston then draws a direct connection between this Arthur / Artaois figure and some of the written versions of Arthur's tale by Marie De France and Chrestien de Troyes.

I have to say, I was initially rather worried about this conflation of God and man, mostly because of Sjoestedt's pronouncement that "There may be analogies between gods and a hero; but there is no transition".[21] In other words, the Bear God Artaois does not suddenly become the very mortal, very human Arthur. However, Arthur is more than just a human. He is a figure of legend and far more than a mortal. John Sharkey disagrees with Sjoestedt and claims "The easy movement between the human warrior hero and his otherworldly archetype, the sun god, is a common practice in every kind of Celtic story."[22] Although not directly naming Artaois, Starkey states that this is definitely the case with Arthur:

Arthur may well have been a historical figure, a sixth-century British military leader; but his importance is as a mythical hero: an important solar warrior. He is the most popular and the most romantic of the Celtic sun heroes.[23]

Philip and Stephanie Carr-Gomm draw a similar comparison,

where "The Arthurian legend, like a golden thread, connects the most sophisticated post-Christian forms of Druidic understanding with the very roots of Druidry in the Celtic and pre-Celtic past".[24] The pre-Celtic past they are referring to here is the bear cults of central Europe mentioned in the previous chapter, where the bear is "*the* primal"[25] totem of humanity. It was from those early bear cults that the figure of Artaois emerged. In that sense, it is not such a stretch to see how Arthur may have evolved from Artaois.

For me, this correlation between Arthur and Artaois feels particularly potent. We can see many of the echoes of Artaois' characteristics as tribal god, "father, nurturer, protector of the tribe, warrior, magician and craftsman"[26] in our conception of Arthur, the archetypal protector of England. He also correlates with Artaois' role as a protector of society and social norms, trying to ensure chivalric behaviour and wanting to bring renewal to his kingdom though finding the Holy Grail. In fact, the only element which doesn't really fit with our characterisation of Arthur is that of magician, although it is worth noting that these elements have become distilled into the figure of Merlin. However, it was when I considered Arthur's death that the full connection between Arthur and Artaois became clear to me. While many tales focus on his death, there are also whispers that Arthur is "not dead but only sleeping on the isle of Avalon".[27] In other words, he entered into some form of bearish hibernation and is ready to return when England needs him. For me, this gave some legitimacy to Rolleston's theory that Arthur and Artaois had become blended and I decided to follow that path.

By getting to know Arthur better I felt I could get to know Artaois. This, however, proved incredibly difficult, with a firm understanding of Arthur being as elusive as the Holy Grail. As John and Caitlin so eloquently put it in their excellent book *The Complete King Arthur: Many Faces, One Hero*:

...who exactly is King Arthur? This question is asked with increasing regularity, both in media and in an outpouring of books, articles and academic studies on the subject published every year. Yet it seems that few, if any, of those who ask the question can agree upon the answer. [28]

As the years go by, more and more theories emerge about who exactly Arthur was and many places have laid claim to being the sites mentioned in Arthurian legend. There are many different traditions and numerous versions of the same stories. The Matthews' explore many of these different Arthurs, both real and legendary, but trying to find Artaois in the centre of these stories is as impossible as finding the 'real' Arthur himself. Bogged down in reading, I decided to head to the place where Arthur/Artaois is apparently waiting for us, just 30 miles south east of Wild Place, where the bears have come back.

Visiting Avalon, or Glastonbury as it is better known these days, is always incredibly special. From the moment I see the Tor in the far distance, my heart leaps with joy and I become filled with excitement (which normally evaporates as I try to find parking). There simply isn't another place like it. Glastonbury has a very special energy and numerous connections to Arthur. Not only is it Arthur's final resting place, with his supposed grave sitting within the grounds of Glastonbury Abbey, but it is also where Arthur found Excalibur. Joseph of Arimathea is said to have dropped the Holy Grail into the Chalice Well, which is why it runs red, and then planted his staff on Wearyall Hill, where it became the Holy Thorn.

But is Artaois there? My first experience of bear energy in Glastonbury actually happened in Glastonbury Town Hall during an Eisteddfod. I was watching the performance on the stage when the image of a bear seemed to lumber out of the stage and down through the hall towards me. She was very much consistent with my image of Artio and wasn't in any way threatening. She just walked off and through the space. With this experience fresh in my memory, I began my search at Glastonbury Abbey, which is right next door to the Town Hall.

Amongst the ruined walls of the choir lie the supposed graves of Arthur and Guinevere. While I have always found visiting this site to be a really intense experience, if they are Arthur's remains then they are certainly that of a mortal man and not the Bear God I was seeking. In fact, there is a sense of oppression connected to the grave: "The Welsh believed that Arthur was not dead and would return in their hour of need. King Henry II did his best to prove that Arthur was indeed deceased and was not about to return and restore a rival British line of kings ... [which] certainly accounts for his personal interest in the supposed discovery of Arthur's bones in 1191 at Glastonbury Abbey...".[29] Ironically then, the grave in Glastonbury was used to quash the sense that Arthur was more than a man, that he was dead rather than waiting to return.

I turned my attention to Glastonbury's most obviously mystical feature; the Tor. The Tor is far more than simply a tourist attraction with a good view. It is a profoundly magical site. It is incredibly potent in terms of its energy and is believed by many to be the entrance to the Celtic underworld, or Annwn. Although the entrance to the underworld has associations with both Gwynn Ap Nudd and Avallach, I felt that it was far more likely that Artaois was hibernating in the Annwn than close to the Abbey, so visited the Tor to see if I could find him there. In a short meditation on the slopes of the Tor, I did briefly find Artaois and he was very different to Artio. Rather than presenting as a bear, Artaois was a man dressed in a full bearskin, as if he were a human hidden within the folds of a bear's body. Very much a leader, Artaois also seemed to embody the sage and nurturing aspects I had expected, but there was also a fierceness and resilience to him. The experience was not very long, it was more of a glimpse than a full encounter, but it certainly gave me a sense of who I was tracking. When I reflected on the meditation, I suddenly became aware that he reminded me of another figure from a place with strong Arthurian connections which had I visited previously.

In 2017 I visited Tintagel in Cornwall for the first time. My journey there had been incredibly difficult and I had arrived somewhat agitated. I began to explore the site of Tintagel Castle, curated by English Heritage, and will freely admit that I was very distracted at the start of my visit, however, arriving on the wild and rocky coastline was an awe-inspiring experience. As I climbed the steep steps up to the Island courtyard, my worries simply melted away. Being on the heights of Tintagel is a very potent, elemental experience and soon I was exploring the ruins surrounded and supported by Earth, Sea, and Sky.

High in the north east corner of the island I found something which took my breath away; a larger than life-sized sculpture of a male figure called *Gallos*, the Cornish word for power. The figure is standing solidly on the earth, leaning on his sword. His head is slightly inclined and his face swathed in a hood which is topped by a crown. Further down the sculpture, parts

Gallos Statue by Sue Knott

29

of the body and cloak are missing so that observers can see the landscape through it. I was intrigued by the sense that this was a figure which both was and was not there. Perhaps the more pressing question was who the statue is meant to be: is it Arthur or is it one of the more earthly kings from this area? When questioned by a journalist, property manager of the site Matt Ward responded "It's up to you, it's up to the visitors to decide. You can interpret it how you like."[30]

Having tracked the bear god through his connection with Arthur, the *Gallos* statue has become, for me, a statue of Artaois. Rather like the statue of Artio in Bern, *Gallos* presents a figure which is both human and more than human, of this world and yet otherworldly. The fact that *Gallos* stands at Tintagel also feels appropriate. This potential representation of Artaois stands on the spot where Geoffrey of Monmouth tells us his energy manifested itself in the legendary birth of Uther Pendragon's son. The missing parts of the statue force the observer to 'fill in the gaps' of the figure, imagining his cloak swirling around him on the tempest struck headland. That, for me, is the perfect analogy for Artaois, where I have had to use my imagination, my understanding, to try fill in the gaps about who he is. In that sense, *Gallos* brought me to understand Artaois both is and is not Arthur.

Tracking Artio

Artio's presence in Britain has somewhat unclear foundations. While Patricia Monaghan states "Artio was known in Britain and Gaul",[31] Kathy Jones proposes that Britain had a different bear goddess: "... the race of Partholon came to Ireland. I name these people as followers of Artha ... who is the Great She Bear of the heavens ... She is connected to Earth Mother Ertha or Eortha, to Ars, Artio and Artemis Callisto also a Bear Mother. Artha is the true Mother of the British hero/king Arthur, whose name comes from Art Vawr meaning Heavenly Bear".[32] Ireland seems to play an important, if enigmatic, role in this story:

> Although the cult of the bear in Celtic Ireland can only be
> inferred from fragmentary evidence, the bear's importance is
> suggested by such common surnames as Mathghamna, Son
> of a Bear.[33]

With little evidence for Artio in Britain, I turned to the
archaeological finds to see if I could find any clues there. When
discussing Artio, Green comments upon "several jet bears
[found] in North Britain: a York bear-pendant was found in a
fourth century AD burial; and at Malton a child was buried with
a tiny jet bear amulet too small to be a toy".[34] Hannah O'Regan's
work extends this description and gives a tantalising link back
to Artio:

> There are rare three-dimensional figurines of bears from
> Roman Britain, including a Roman copper alloy figure of a
> bear holding a small figure (possibly a child) in its jaws ...
> This was suggested to be a funerary figure, which could link
> it with the seven jet bears from late Roman children's graves
> and sites of cultic activity in Colchester, York and Malton ...
> Parallels for these bears in Britain have also been found in
> Trier and Cologne.[35]

I found this is particularly resonant as Trier is very close to
Ernzen and Weilerbach where I began tracing the archaeological
evidence for Artio.

Reflecting on the nature of the small bear figures found in
the graves, I wondered if this linked to the sense of Artio being a
goddess of rebirth: by burying a loved one with a bear, was there
a hope that they would be reborn? I also found it incredibly
potent that these figures all seem to have a strong connection
to children, either depicting them or being found in children's

graves. This really gives the sense of a Bear Goddess being a protector of children, a fierce mother who looks after her cubs.

At somewhat of a loss as to how I could track Artio further, I mentally retraced my steps back to Glastonbury where I had potentially had an encounter with the Goddess. I decided to contact a friend who was a Priestess of Avalon to see if she knew of any practitioners who specifically worked with Bear Goddesses. I soon found myself connecting with Louisa Potter who lives in the north west highlands of Scotland. I asked her when she had first begun working with the spirit of the bear. She told me "Bear first started to show herself to me around 2012. At this point I had completed my Priestess of Avalon training but was unclear what my role as a Priestess was in the world. I didn't feel called to anything in particular and was drifting. As is often the case with spiritual awakenings, it came when I was having a difficult time with family life and my role as a mother was being questioned. Around this time a friend suggested I watch the Disney film *Brave* which is set in the Highlands. After initially dismissing the suggestion, I watched it and became obsessed with the Bear Mother archetype at the centre of the story. By a lovely piece of serendipity, I also discovered the books *Bear Witnessing* and *The Last Bear* by Mandy Haggith around the same time. The latter was inspirational for me, exploring the intertwined stories of the last bear in Scotland and the last bear shaman at the time when the Christian church was establishing itself. I wanted to get in touch with Mandy to tell her how moved I was by her writing and she invited me to meet her at her home in the Scottish Highlands. I had a long-standing love for the Highlands and was planning a walking holiday there around the time, so I ended up visiting Mandy and fell in love with Assynt and Bear Magic."

"From my first afternoon in Assynt I knew that Bear was the heart of my magical path and that this place was where I should be living. It was a real turning point. Mandy said to me that 'we won't get bears back on this land until we have the bear

Priestesses back'. My response was visceral: 'Yup that is my path' I thought to myself! And that is what my life has been about ever since. I became a regular visitor to Assynt and had what I believe were 'uploads' from the bears who sleep beneath the landscape here. I spent every scrap of time I had writing or exploring the land. I also spent time learning about the bears that walk this earth, mainly brown, black and polar bears, reading books on their lives and biology and their part in our human history. Basically, I was soaking up anything bearish that I could find. I didn't know what form all these ideas would take in the long run but began sharing them in the world. I eventually moved to Assynt in 2017."

Louisa's work with the Priestesses of Avalon have led her to create a range of workshops and techniques to help others connect with the spirit of the bear, called The Temple of Ursa (https://www.bearfootwalkingtempleofursa.com/). "In the long run I would like to open a physical temple space where I could bring groups to work with the landscape and Bear energy. It would be something very in harmony with the land and this community. There's no point having a temple if it doesn't serve both the local community and visitors", she told me. "I also would like it to be a place where spirituality and ecological activism meet; there must be real world action to follow spiritual connection. For me that's one of the strongest qualities of Bear; she dances across the starry sky, the place of dreams and spirit, but also leaves strong solid pawprints in the earth, the realm of grounded manifest action. She can hold both things at once and moves between these two extremes in strong rhythms like a great heartbeat. That is her strength."

The work of The Temple of Ursa is underpinned by four principles called the four Paw Prints, all based on lessons Louisa has learned while working with the bear energy in Assynt. The first two Paw Prints explore the relationship between the human body and the world around us; *Stretching to our Wild Expanses* encourages us to sharpen and use our senses, while *Bare Bear Witnessing* explores the human connection to the wild landscape. The third Paw Print, *Sleeping in the Cave of the Grandmother Bear*, focusses on our relationship with the dream and spirit worlds. Louisa developed this principle based on a visit to Inchnadamph Bone Caves near Assynt. She told me "In the past hundred years cavers and scientists have discovered a huge collection of animal bones in these caves including lynx, arctic fox and reindeer. They have found bones from three individual bears, one of which is from a polar bear and is about 11,000 years old. The spirit of bear has been here since before the last ice age."

The final Paw Print is the *Council of the Bear Clans*, which focuses on our role within community. This Paw Print seemed particularly potent to me, considering the number of people I had met on my journey towards Artio and Artaois. "My connection to Avalon and Somerset is about the community" Louisa told me. "People go there for spiritual learning and support, so it's a great way to make connections, as our meeting has proved!" I found it interesting to note that Beth Wildwood, who also works so closely with bears, also spent time in Somerset when she was younger.

Along with the Paw Prints, Louisa has created a Wheel of She-Bears which is rooted in the Celtic Wheel of the Year. "For me I began to feel this Wheel of She-Bears as I became more familiar with the Highland landscape and the way of bears. It wasn't a conscious or forced thing, it just made sense and the She Bears came through more strongly with each season." The Wheel has Ursa at its heart, but explores each festival through a distinct incarnation of the She-Bear. For example, the new beginnings celebrated at Imbolc are exemplified through the emergence of the New Cub, deep from within its winter cave. The connections explored in the Wheel led Louisa to develop additional workshops at The Temple of Ursa: "During my time training and working as Priestess of Avalon, I was drawn to the Goddess Arta, who sits on the Wheel of Avalon at Spring Equinox. Her element is fire and one of her animals is Bear. This connection led me to train in fire walking with Oona MacFarlane at her base near Loch Lomond. For me there is a strong connection between Bear and fire. It's that very creative energy of spring, emerging out of the cave and into the light, really letting your creative self burn brightly." Louisa also found a connection between the energy of the Water Bear at the Summer Solstice and glass walking. "I feel that Bear energy is very much about creating change in the real world, leaving our pawprint. Both glass and fire walking are empowerment tools which work in the body to allow us to manifest change in the world."

Despite Louisa telling me that she didn't have a strong connection to Artio in particular, much of her work with the spirit of Bear has illuminated my approach to the Goddess. In fact, she encapsulated Artio for me in her phrase "she dances across the starry sky, the place of dreams and spirit, but also leaves strong solid pawprints in the earth, the realm of grounded manifest action". Louisa's work at the Temple of Ursa, with her aim to "use She-Bear energy to heal and support people in their lives" seems the perfect manifestation of Artio's energy in Britain, with the strong, protective earth mother providing guidance and inspiration for those who continue to seek her.

At the end of my explorations in the UK, I was developing a clearer sense of both Artaois and Artio. Following the track that Artaois was "father, nurturer, protector of the tribe, warrior, magician and craftsman"[36] led to the sense that the stories of Artaois and King Arthur "ultimately blended into one".[37] As such, he became emblematic of a strong leader, combining skill as a warrior with the wisdom and magic often associated with the figure of Merlin. Through this association, Artaois became "the most popular and the most romantic of the Celtic sun heroes"[38] strongly associated with the harvests bought by successful rulership, notably trade and commerce. Artio was a vegetation Goddess, clearly overseeing the abundance and harvests of the natural world. She is strongly maternal, even protecting her children through the process of death and rebirth. Her role as a Goddess of various realms, both the spirit and apparent worlds, is encapsulated in Louisa Potter's acknowledgement that "she dances across the starry sky, the place of dreams and spirit, but also leaves strong solid pawprints in the earth, the realm of grounded manifest action".

Having explored the Wheel of She-Bears with Louisa, I wondered if more light could be shed on Artio and Artaois by taking a syncretic approach, exploring their similarities to other manifestations of Bear Gods and Goddesses in different cultures. As such, my next journey took me around the world.

Chapter 3

Pawprints around the World

Gathering the She-Bears

It had become clear, both through my initial research into bear worship in Europe and through my exploration of bears in Britain, that there were a number of other figures who were beginning to influence my journey. For example, to continue tracking Artaois I had been led to see him both through and within the figure of Arthur. Similarly, conversations about Artio had ended up with Goddesses such as Ursa and Arta taking precedent. Rather than fight this tendency, I decided to embrace it and develop a syncretic view of both Artio and Artaois, exploring them through their associations with other, similar deities. However, before I started looking at them comparatively, I wanted to see if I could go back to the very beginning, to find the primeval, mythical cave from which the bear deities emerged.

The seminal work on bears around the world is *The Sacred Paw* by Paul Shepherd and Barry Sanders, which gives the most comprehensive overview of, as it says on the title page, "the bear in nature, myth and literature". From the very beginning, Shepherd and Sanders explore the sense of connection between bears and humans and suggest that connection is because we sense that bears are very like us: "Watching them explore their environments, we recognise a consciousness [in bears] somewhat like our own. We have an uncanny feeling that beneath the fur is a man."[1] They suggest that this sense of a deep, primal connection between bears and humans is preserved in an ancient story that has been told in different forms by cultures around the world, a story which "shows why both bears and people are part animal, part human":[2] the story of the Bear Mother.

The Bear Mother story involves a young woman who is

abducted and taken to a cave far from her tribal lands. Once there, it is revealed that her abductors are actually divine bears, keeping their human form when in the cave but donning skins and becoming bears when they venture into the outside world. The young woman is married to the son of the chief, known as the Bear Husband, and they have two sons, who are half human and half bear. However, shortly after, the young woman's family come to find her. They ritually kill the Bear Husband before taking the Bear Mother and her sons back to their village and it is from the Bear Sons that the rest of humanity is descended. This ancient story explores the ideas that bears are human underneath and also establishes humanity is descended from bears, giving a common ancestor in the Bear Mother. Shepherd and Sanders take this idea further, showing how this tale developed into something more potent: "The Bear Mother may also be the first great mythopoetic mother of all life (the first external incarnation among animals of our personal mothers), prior in history and deeper in the psyche than her humanlike expression".[3]

Their suggestion here is startling; that humanity's first understanding of a Goddess is through the avatar of a female bear. This takes us back to the statue of Artio in Bern, where it was originally the bear which represented the Goddess, the human figure being added later. In this sense, Artio becomes more than simply a mid-European figure from a bear cult. She becomes a potent expression of humanity's earliest worship of a Goddess and a universal mother. She is not A Goddess but THE Goddess, a manifestation of the very first female deity worshipped by humans. As such, rather than using this chapter to see Artio in the light of other Goddesses, as I suggested above, it would be more accurate to say that I will be looking at other Goddesses as incarnations of Artio, herself an incarnation of "the first great mythopoetic mother of all life".[4]

Perhaps the most obvious place to find echoes of Artio is in another Bear Goddess mentioned in inscriptions in Bern:

Andarta, a Goddess of the Vocontii tribe. While it has been suggested that her name means "well-fixed, staying firm",[5] Andarta clearly shares the root of her name, 'Art', with Artio. However, her name contains the "intensive prefix ande-," meaning that Andarta isn't just a Bear Goddess but is the "Great Bear".[6] There are eight surviving inscriptions to Andarta in France and Switzerland (three more than there are for Artio) and in five of those inscriptions, Andarta is referred to as 'August', which shows her as being of particular "sacredness and potency and indicates that her cult was made official in the Roman pantheon, probably towards the end of the 1st c. AD."[7] While there are some suggestions that Andarta was a Goddess of fertility[8] or the wilderness,[9] both Patricia Monaghan and Marie Louise Sjoestedt state that Andarta was "known as a goddess of war".[10] This is certainly at odds with the placid bear on the plinth in Bern, suggesting a different side to the Bear Goddess, although Monaghan's suggestion seems to rely purely on "the basis of her name to be similar to the war goddess Andraste."[11] However, surely the closeness of morphology in Andarta and Artio's names, located in the same geographical area, suggest a greater link between the two Goddesses than connecting Andarta with an Icenic war Goddess from across the sea. James McKillop suggests that Andarta "may be a counterpart of Artio".[12] Personally, that is how I have come to view Andarta, as another echo of the primal Bear Mother which happened in the same region, or the same manifestation given a different, more loaded name.

Another Goddess who is frequently linked to Artio is from the south-eastern Mediterranean. Monaghan states that "In function as well as name, Artio resembles the Greek Artemis, also depicted as a bear."[13] This comparison seems a little straightforward. To begin with, Artio's name may be similar to Artemis, but, coming from different cultures, the names do not share the same meaning. 'Art' means bear in the Celtic languages but the Ancient Greek word for bear is 'ἄρκτος' or 'arktos', which is clearly not the root of Artemis' name. In fact, there is still some question over what Artemis name actually means:

> Although the exact meaning of the name Artemis is not known for certain, the Roman writer Strabo suggests a meaning for it in his writings, saying that she made people 'Artemeas' which means Safe and Sound. Plato suggests that Artemis took her name from her healthy (artemes) and well-ordered nature, and possibly due to her disliking sexual intercourse (to aroton misesasa).[14]

Similarly, stating that Artemis was depicted as a bear is not quite right. Artemis was a Goddess of "wild animals, the hunt, and vegetation, and of chastity and childbirth"[15] and, as such, had a number of animals associated with her, such as boar and deer, alongside bears. However, while Monaghan's comparison seemed straightforward, the above list does provide some interesting links with between the two. It is clear that Artemis' role as a vegetation goddess links her to the "Vegetationsgöttin"[16] of Bern, while Artemis' role as a goddess of childbirth connects her to the protective Bear-Mother, Artio. The most notable difference between the two goddesses, however, is in Artemis' connection to the hunt. There is no evidence to suggest Artio was a goddess of hunting in any of the surviving archaeology, although it is possible that the story of the Bear Mother, with its hunting and ritualised killing of the Bear Husband, could connect the two.

Artemis' deep connection with bears can be seen most clearly in two instances, the first being one of her places of worship. In her book on Artemis, Sorita D'Este outlines the history and rituals undertaken in the name of the goddess at the temple of Artemis Brauronia, also known as The Parthenon of the Bear Maidens, in the historic region of Attica. The site seems to have been a focus for worship to protect women during childbirth and for girls up to puberty, and was in use in the 9th and 8th century BCE, although there is evidence it was used as early as the Neolithic age. Images of worship at the temple show young girls dressed as Arktoi, or She-Bears, apparently at the command of Artemis herself:

> This custom [of dressing up as bears] has its origins in a story which tells of the killing of a tame she-bear who frequented the sanctuary. A young girl teased the she-bear, which became agitated. It attacked the girl and ripped out her eye. Subsequently the girl's brothers took revenge on the bear, killing it. Artemis retaliated and sent a plague to the sanctuary. In desperation the people of Brauron consulted an Oracle and were told that the only way to appease the goddess was for the girls to take on the role of the she-bear in a mystery play.[17]

The dance of the young female worshippers clearly signified more than simply honouring the tame bear killed in the temple. In many ways, the dance became a symbol of transformation "from the wild and untamed status of childhood to that of a respectable life as a married woman."[18] The dance of the Arktoi shares some thematic similarities with the other connection between Artemis and bears; the story of her votary, Callisto:

> In one version of the myth, Artemis discovers that Callisto is pregnant. For copulating with men, Artemis transforms Callisto into her most familiar bestial incarnation, the side of her that is most unchaste, most unvirginlike – a she-bear. In another version, Zeus impregnates Callisto. Hera, Zeus' jealous wife, punishes Callisto by turning her into a bear; again, the bear is seen as the fallen, bestial side of Callisto.[19]

Like the symbolism of the dance at Brauron, the tales of Callisto conflict somewhat with the sense of Artio as humanity's first incarnation of a mother goddess. Callisto's transformation into a form seen as the most wild and bestial implies a moving away from the idea that humans and bears were closely related. It suggests that the Greeks had developed a moral continuum where humans were at one end and bears, as representative of the wilderness, were at the other. This seems completely opposite to Shepherd and Sanders' suggestions of a deep connection between humans and bears, upon which so much of the early worship of bears seems to be based. While there does seem to be some connection between Artio and Artemis, there are also areas where they clearly diverge.

However, there is an interesting echo of the Bear Mother story in the heart of the Callisto tale, which deserves further scrutiny. In this tale, Callisto's son, Arcas, is found hunting his own mother. "In both versions, Arcas, the son of Callisto, hunts his bear mother and pursues her to Mount Lycaeus, Zeus' sacred ground. To save her from matricide or as punishment for that trespass, Zeus fixes them both in the heavens as the constellations Great Bear and Little Bear, circling on the Axis of the heavens."[20] This reminds us the ancient tale of the Bear Mother, although this time it augments the story with a new and beautiful element: the transformation of Callisto and her son into the constellations Ursa Major and Ursa Minor, the Great Bear and the Little Bear. I will discuss the connection between bears and the constellations more fully later in the chapter.

Because she too is a goddess of the hunt, the Roman goddess Diana is often linked to bears and has been considered to be a bear goddess. However, this seems to be mostly through her associations with Artemis and there seems to be no specific links between Diana and bears. However, it is worth mentioning here that the Latin word for bear, Ursa, has particular potency. It is, obviously, the name of the constellations Ursa Major and

Minor, as well as being the name for the bear spirit worked with by Louisa Potter at the Temple of Ursa in Scotland, a place for honouring the "Spirit of She Bear in Brigid's Isles".[21]

Another bear goddess whose name began to appear in my research is that of Artha, sometimes called Arta. Kathy Jones lists her as "the Mother of Fire ... that is in all stars and in the centre of the Earth. She is the fire on the hearth in our homes and in our hearts. ... She is the fire that brings light, warmth and life to all the world".[22] This link to fire is something I had seen before, in Louisa Potter's barefoot walking work at The Temple of Ursa, where she runs fire walking experiences for those trying to get close to bear energy. This connection with fire means that Artha is traditionally placed on the Wheel of the Year at Ostara, the Spring Equinox, also called Alban Eilir. Caroline Gully-Lir suggests that "Artha is so ancient that only distant memory of Her remains"[23], although Jones suggests that there are some remains left behind by her worshippers, the "great chambered long barrows and mounds"[24] still found across Britain. This suggestion is incredibly interesting, after all, long barrows could be seen as replicas of the denning or hibernation spaces bears seek out in the winter months. As mentioned earlier, bears are deeply connected to the underworld, death and rebirth, so perhaps putting the remains of the dead in such a space was a way of putting them in the care of the bear mother.

There are many other bear goddesses from cultures across the world. Many of them seem to have been lost, or little information exists about them, rather like Artio. For example, in Hungary there are traces of Ildiko, a goddess of the hunt and the forests,[25] while in Finland there are tales of Mielikki, a healing bear goddess who travels beyond the moon,[26] about whom there is some more information later in this chapter. However, there may be one bear goddess who has been hiding in plain sight: the Celtic goddess Brighid or Bridget. Clues to Bridget's link to bears begin with her name: "The source of the name Bridget is the stem word for "bear"; she is a Celtic fire goddess and Christian saint. Linked to the same word origins are "bright" and "shine", reminding us of Jung's assertion that there is a bear with glowing eyes deep in the human unconscious".[27] Similarly, both Bridget and bears are associated with hearths. It appears that Bridget's Swedish counterpart also had a connection with bears: "During the Catholic era St. Birgitta became guardian of the bear. Hunters turned to her so that she would keep her bears under control... St Birgitta in English would become Bridget or Bride".[28] Shepherd and Sanders deepen the suggestion that Brigid is a bear goddess by illustrating the range of bear festivals which take place on February 2nd, celebrated in the Celtic tradition as Bride's Day or Imbolc and the Christian festival of Candlemas. This is the time of year that bear cubs would leave their dens, "Entering the world anew"[29] with their mother. As a result, bear festivals are found across Europe. It is that tradition, of the bear leaving its cave, which gave birth to the American tradition of Groundhog Day. Conversely, in the Swedish tradition of St Birgitta, it is the day the bear goes into their den, not the day they come out, which is marked: "October 7th in Telemark is Britemesse, in memory of St. Birgitta of Sweden. It is supposedly the day the bear collects heather and moss and goes to his winter den".[30] Similar to the connection between Artaois and Arthur, the association between Artio and Bridget helps to throw a different light on our assumptions about our most ancient goddess.

Gathering the Bear Sons

To begin our exploration of Artaois, we have to go back to the story of the Bear Mother and the important role played by her divine husband. When he realises that the brothers are coming for the Bear Mother, the Bear Husband knows that he must die and teaches his sons how he must be hunted and honoured to ensure that the human tribe enjoys good luck after his death. This is an incredibly benign action towards humanity, considering that it is they who will kill him. Shephard and Sanders note that "The Bear God dies for the welfare of people, exacting atonement and propitiation from the hunters."[31] Again, we get the sense of the Bear God as "protector of the tribe"[32] here, ensuring that humans continue to enjoy good fortune, even if they kill him.

The idea that there are set routines and rituals in how bears must be hunted and killed was not just confined to storytelling. In 1926, Alfred Irving Hallowell published an article called *Bear Ceremonialism in the Northern Hemisphere* in which he outlined the ways bears are hunted in indigenous societies around the globe. In doing so, he found a large number of similarities in how the hunt was approached, ultimately suggesting that they all stem from the same source, where "a bear cult was one of the characteristic features of an ancient Boreal culture"[33] which later became international. For example, he notes that "The favorite time to hunt the beast is toward the end of the winter, or in the early spring, while snow is still on the ground"[34], with the bear often being roused from its den and killed with a ceremonial weapon while still drowsy and disoriented. The hunters often approached the animal in an almost apologetic, conciliatory manner, referring to the bear by names which showed kinship and affection, such as "Cousin ... Grandfather or Grandmother"[35], "Four-legged human", "Old man" or "Elder brother".[36] Once killed, parts of the bear (usually the skull, pelt and heart) became trophies and a large feast of bear meat would be held in honour of the hunter who killed the bear and of the bear itself. In some cultures, "the [slaughtered] bear is petitioned not to allow the spirits of other bears to be angry with the hunter or asked to inform other members of its species how well it was treated, so that they will desire to share a similar fate"[37]. In his work, Hallowell noted that no other animal has such elaborate rituals associated with it, particularly in terms of the conciliatory way it is treated. While this may lead us to believe that there is something otherworldly about the animal, Hallowell made clear that the bear in itself was in no way a god, rather a creature special to and under the control of particular deities.

While we may begin to sense links between the figure of Artaois, the Bear Husband and the hunted bears discussed by Hallowell, it's is also worth noting that the cultures the latter investigated are far further north than the one from which Artaois emerged. There is no sense of the Celtic or pre-Celtic cultures in his work. But that does not mean that we should simply rule out a connection. In the sense that Artaois can be seen as a solar deity, that he, or an animal sacred to him, would be ritually hunted and killed makes a connection to Sir James Frazer's idea of "the Killing of the Divine King"[38]. The fact that the hunts used to take place in late winter, just before the bear emerged from its winter den, also suggests that the ceremony had a sense of renewal about it, where the ritualised killing and conciliatory nature of the hunt marked a sense of hope of things to come. In that sense, perhaps Artaois does draw us back to this ancient custom as being a beneficent spirit who nurtures and nourishes his tribe from deep within the forests.

However, while the Bear Husband marks one potential track towards Artaois, another route to him can be found by following the Bear Mother's children, rather than her husband. Shepherd and Sanders note that, over time, the Bear Mother story began to die away and the focus changed to the daring adventure of the Bear Son. The story of the Bear Son begins in much the same way as that of the Bear Mother, with a human female being taken by a bear into a den and the couple having a child. However, in this adaptation of the story, the mother and child escape and return to their village, where the Bear Son grows in strength and prowess. When he reaches maturity, the Bear Son begins a long quest which eventually leads him into the depths of the underworld. After a series of trials, the Bear Son returns home from his adventures, seemingly having escaped death, with riches and prizes to suit his new stature. In many ways what Shepherd and Sanders describe is a prototype of the Hero's Journey, the underpinning structure of many of our core myths and beliefs popularised by Joseph Campbell. The effect of this shift of focus, from Bear Mother to Bear Son, according to Shepherd and Sanders, was to have a profound effect on the human belief:

> In a sense there has been no more crucial shift in the turbulent history of the past ten millennia than this new emphasis and allegory ... Thus do the traces of the bear as the perfect and wild mother, rearing her sons, furnish the Old European early agriculture with its ideals of the renewing and protecting Bear Mother... But in time, Old Europe was swamped and overlaid by Indo-European cultures with their celebration not of the mother but of the son. As the warrior patriarchs shaped the world of male power and masculine ideals, the nurturing feminine image became subordinate to that of the wonderful son who renewed himself underground.[39]

This shift from the more primal female bear deity, connected closely to the natural world, to the male bear deity, who seems to have dominion over human affairs, is a characteristic I found in my initial exploration of Artio and Artaois in Europe. It suggests that Artaois is a Bear Son figure, a child of Artio rather than her husband and also aligns him with the mythological and literary heroes that emerged from the early Bear Son tale, characters such as Hercules, Orpheus, Odysseus and, in Celtic culture, King Arthur.

Another Bear Son, one from northern Europe who left his mark English Literature, was also literally named after a bear: Beowulf, whose name translates as "Bee Wolf", a kenning for "Bear"[40]. As a Bear Son archetype, Beowulf goes on a series of thrilling quests where he rids Heorot Hall of the monster Grendel, swims to the depths of a lake from where he seemingly returns from the dead, before fighting a dragon deep within an earthen barrow. Within the tale we not only find a hero with the strength of a bear, who is capable of journeying into the underworld, but one who is also kind and beneficent: "The ethical values are manifestly the Germanic code of loyalty to chief and tribe and vengeance to enemies. Yet ... Beowulf himself seems more altruistic than other Germanic heroes"[41]. This sense of beneficence linked to a Bear Son may seem strange to modern readers. After all, the contemporary, brutal Viking warriors were called Berserkers, their name literally means 'the bears shirts'. So why is Beowulf not drawn in this light? While some critics believe that "Beowulf" is a Christian allegory, I'd like to suggest that our conception of bears today is different to that of the Germanic and Celtic peoples who told tales of Beowulf and worshipped Mercury Artaius. When discussing the characteristics of the European Brown Bear, Shepherd and Sanders state that "In general, bears are shy animals that avoid trouble ... The false image of raging ferocity is in part the residue of spectacles in the plazas and 'bear-gardens' of Europe and America, where bears were goaded into fights with bulls or dogs; it also derives from the fierceness with which bears defend their lives and space when surrounded by frontiersmen, hunted by ranchers with dogs, or crowded by tourists and hikers"[42]. It seems to me that trying to frame Artaois as a blood-thirsty warrior does a disservice to those who worshipped him. While there is evidence to suggest the Celts connected bears and warriors, there is also evidence to show that bears were considered as mystical creatures of rebirth from the deep forest. Artaois, through his connection with Mercury and with the figure of the Bear Son, certainly has strength and the potential to attack but is not a "Berserker".

While his association with Mercury may mean Artaois was not a bloodthirsty warrior, it could lead us to another deity who can cast light on Artaois' characteristics. While researching bears on the OBOD website, I found the statement that "Artaius had also been identified with another Welsh figure, named Gwydion"[43], although the connection was not expanded upon. Initially, I was suspicious of this association, with Gwydion seeming nothing like the Bear Son figures I had found in Arthur and Beowulf. Being described as "a master of magic and poetry and a somewhat dubious character"[44] and "the great magician and trickster of the Fourth Branch of the Welsh Mabinogi"[45], Gwydion seemed the very antithesis of the Bear God I was tracking. However, it was then that I remembered that Mercury, the only direct association we have for Artaois, was himself a wily trickster. Rather than dismissing the association, I decided to dig deeper.

And it is true, the character of Gwydion portrayed early on in the Fourth Branch of *The Mabinogion* does seem to be of "dubious character", enabling, with magic, the rape of Goewin by Gilfaethwy. As their punishment, Gwydion and Gilfaethwy are transformed into a series of animals who must "live together and mate with each other",[46] assuming the characteristics of the animals they become. Over three years the brothers become deer, boars and wolves, but never bears, possibly because bears were not living wild in Wales at this stage. However, elsewhere in the text, Gwydion is described as "the best storyteller in the world"[47] and clearly uses his magic to protect and improve the life of his young nephew, Lleu. Gwydion tricks his sister, Lleu's mother, into naming and arming the boy and even creates Lleu a wife, Blodeuedd, from flowers. Reading the Fourth Branch, I recalled some of the words Julius Caesar used when describing the Celtic relationship with Mercury: "they declare him the inventor of all arts, the guide for every road and journey".[48] It is Gwydion's magic and his poetry which make him the master "of all arts" and he can certainly be seen as a protective guide to Lleu. Gregory Wright makes further connections, drawing similarities between Gwydion and Merlin, as well as outlining how Gwydion used his skills with language and riddles to defeat Arawn, Lord of the Welsh Otherworld, Annwn.[49]. Fighting the Lord of the realm of the dead, even in a game of wits, and winning feels akin to the journey to the underworld made by the Bear Son figure.

On balance, it is difficult to develop the link between Gwydion and Artaois as there seems to be little direct correlation. However, the association is useful to remind us that Artaois likely had artistic and magical qualities for those who worshipped him. The degree to which he was a trickster God is difficult to assess but it's quite pleasing to think of him conjuring in the woodland and tripping up the humans who came too close!

One of the places I felt most deeply connected to the spirit of the bear was when I travelled to North Carolina in the USA. I was lucky enough to stay close to the Blue Ridge Mountains and the whole area is imbued with the energy of the black bear. I decided to explore the Native American understanding of bears and was lucky enough to find the work of Jessica Dawn Palmer, who has drawn together Animal Wisdom from across cultures, particularly from her own Native American heritage. What is so interesting is to see the same kind of themes emerge across and between cultures and tribes. For example, there is a strong magical theme in Palmer's exploration of bears, exploring how the Lakota believed that "When bear appeared in a vision to someone, that person became a shaman" and that "bear was the keeper of herb lore, and the primary medicine animal".[50] Similarly, for the Mandan Tribe "grizzlies were associated with protection, plenty and the supernatural",[51] whereas for the Woodland Dakotas, the spirit of dead warriors often took the form of bears, meaning the creature "was equated with death and war".[52] Palmer also ties in the Bear Son's journey to the underworld, but gives it a more psychological edge: "If working with the unconscious, invoke grizzly or brown bears for protection. It can also act as a guide in the murky world of the subconscious".[53]

Finally, I decided to investigate the story of Honey Paw which had been mentioned by Beth Wildwood. The tale can be found in *The Kalevala*, a nineteenth century epic poem which recounts many Finnish myths. Honey Paw is one of many epithets used for Otso, the spirit of all bears, who was born in the sky:

Honey-paw was born in ether,
In the regions of the Moon-land[54]

Rune XLVI of *The Kalevala* goes on to describe how a maiden in the ether scatters wool across the Earth, which is collected by Mielikki, the lady of the forest:

[Mielikki] Took the fragments from the sea-side,
Took the white wool from the waters,
Sewed the hair and wool together,
Laid the bundle in her basket,
Basket made from bark of birch-wood,
Bound with cords the magic bundle;
With the chains of gold she bound it
To the pine-tree's topmost branches.
There she rocked the thing of magic,
Rocked to life the tender baby ...
Thus the young bear well was nurtured,
Thus was sacred Otso cradled
On the honey-tree of Northland,
In the middle of the forest. [55]

Promising not to harm the good people in exchange for being given teeth and claws, Otso is respected by the people of the North, with the rest of Rune XLVI outlining a ceremonial bear feast, much like that described by Hallowell. Otso's spirit returns to sky, in cradle at the top of a pine tree at the summit of a mountain, which will "Rock him to his lasting slumber".[56]

While *The Kalevala* clearly shows the traditions of the ancient bear hunt, Shepherd and Sanders note that the wider work reflects a shift towards stories of heroic valour, more akin to the later story of the Bear Son. With that, they assert that "one sense of the bear gave way to another, and as man gradually assumed the power of the animal, he also gained the courage to repudiate the sacredness of the animals themselves".[57] However, the tale of Honey Paw also provides an interesting connection to another realm of the bears: Otso's birth place, the "ether".

Gathering the Cosmic Bears

Throughout this journey I have focused on the role of bears and bear deities on two planes. The first is the earthly, mortal realm, considering living bears in their environment as well as the role of Artio as a vegetation Goddess and Artaois' influence over human affairs. The second realm is that of the Underworld, whether that be in the sense of death and rebirth or in explorations of the psyche. However, there is a third realm which bears inhabit: that of the sky and stars. It may seem odd that such physically grounded animals should have a cosmic role, but they are indeed seen in the sky, with the constellations of Ursa Major and Ursa Minor dancing around the pole star. It is easy to dismiss the constellations as having their roots in the Greek myth of Callisto, therefore not really having any bearing on our exploration of Artio and Artaois. However, Shepherd and Sanders' work shows that the connection between bears and the stars pre-dates the Greeks, and the connection between the constellations we know as Ursa Major and Minor and bears is common in cultures around the world.

Shepherd and Sanders state that this connection began at a time when the story of the Bear Mother and the ritualised hunting of and feasting upon sacred bears were "the cornerstone of a cosmogenic scheme, a tale of perennial success, and therefore renewal".[58] At this point the cosmology of the bear developed in three realms; "the sky as the home of eternal beings; the earth's surface, that of mortal creatures; the underworld as the place of the dead kinsmen".[59] Interestingly, at this point they tie in the symbol of a tree which also unites the three realms with its roots deep in the earth and its branches in the heavens. Reading this, I was reminded of the statue of Artio in Bern, with the tree reaching up and over the bear, into the sky. For me, this is not just a symbol of the forest home of the bear but shows a connection between Artio and the upper realm of the stars.

Further, Shepherd and Sanders go on to explore how bears have become associated with the constellations known as Ursa Major and Minor in cultures around the world. They discuss how the seven stars of Ursa Major are known as the Seven Bears in Hindu culture and expand on the Finnish tale of Honey Paw to show how the "Ostyaks and Voguls [from northern Russia] tell a story of the earthly bear's origin on a cloud near the Great Bear constellation".[60] They also explore similar stories amongst a variety of tribes from North America. These tales, connected to Ursa Major and Minor, are "a continuing sign of the bear's presence, a weather magistrate and prophet, particularly in connection with palingenesis, the power of renewal and the regeneration of the seasons. The same power is basic to the passage of the bear's own soul and its function as a spiritual envoy between the tumult of life in the ebb and flow of physical being on earth and its eternal pattern, exemplified by the wheeling of the Great Bear in the night sky".[61]

A charm from the *Greek Magical Papyri*, a collection of papyri from Graeco-Roman Egypt, goes further, stating that the bear isn't just "wheeling" in the sky but literally turning the Earth on its axis:

Bear, Bear, you who rule the heaven, the stars, and the whole world; you who make the axis turn and control the whole cosmic system by force and compulsion, I appeal to you...[62]

A similar story comes from rural English culture, with the constellation of Ursa Major being known as Arthur's Plough, being pushed across the night sky by Ursa Minor, the Little Bear, which represents Arthur: "People said that in the dead of the night, if anybody cared to listen, the plough and waggon of the Great and Lesser Bear could be heard turning".[63] This sense of bears driving the cosmos, the cycles of day and night, birth, death, and rebirth is incredibly potent and certainly feel appropriate for the Earth Goddess Artio and her son, governor of the world of men, Artaois. But which is the Great Bear and which the Small?

While many cultures do refer to the Great Bear as 'he', for me Ursa Major represents Artio, an incarnation of the Bear Mother and humanity's first Goddess. She moves across the sky, looking down on us protectively, controlling and governing the seasonal changes which shape all life on Earth. Artaois, then, is the Little Bear, Ursa Minor. He is the Bear Son, coming later in our traditions but sitting higher in the sky, right around the pole star. Although he is smaller, he is no less important. We may see him as following his mother or possibly worrying her, pushing her on, just as some believed Arthur pushed the plough ahead of him.

However, the bears are not alone up there in the sky; they are followed by another constellation, this one known as Boötes, meaning 'Ploughman', the brightest star of which is Arcturus, the "Guardian of the Bear".[64] For some cultures, Boötes is itself the spirit of bear, hunting Elk across the sky, while "In Europe the bear is not the hunter but the hunted. Along with the little bear, she is chased by the human hunter in the constellation of Boötes".[65] High in the sky above us, every night, the ancient hunt of the bear takes place. While some of us may no longer be comfortable with the idea of hunting in the twenty first century, reflecting on Hallowell's observations of the ritual hunting of bears reminds us that it was done with a sense of reverence and respect. In that sense, the nightly hunt above our heads is a potent reminder of the need for us to show respect in all of humanity's dealings with the natural world.

Seen within the context of other bear myths and deities, it is possible to create a more complete picture of Artio and Artaois. A God and Goddess, almost lost to time, are emerging again from the depths of the forest. While it is impossible for us to really know how they were seen by the Celts, by placing Artio and Artaois within the context of other Bear Deities, we have the opportunity to honour the whole history of human bear worship, from the story of the Bear Mother, the bear hunts and ensuing feasts, right through to the story of the Bear Sons and their development into more human heroes. The following descriptions are suggestions of how we can see each of the deities, to make them distinct from each other, to give them their own characters and roles.

Artio, the Goddess honoured with a statue in Bern, depicted as both a human and a bear, is an expression of "the first great mythopoetic mother of all life".[66] She is a vegetation Goddess looking down on the Earth from the constellation of Ursa Major where she turns the seasons. She is a Goddess of the harvest and of plenty. She is our protective mother who, like Artemis, looks after us during childbirth and our youth. Like Artha, whose followers dug the den-like long barrows, Artio also helps guide us into the underworld upon our death and leads us to rebirth. Within the three realms, as Louisa Potter told me, "she dances across the starry sky, the place of dreams and spirit, but also leaves strong solid pawprints in the earth, the realm of grounded manifest action". She guides us into the underworld during times of hardship where we can manifest new ideas, or 'cubs', of our own.

Artaois, the "father, nurturer, protector of the tribe, warrior, magician and craftsman",[67] is a manifestation of the Bear Son, a heroic figure who descends to the underworld and returns, seemingly, from the dead. As such he oversees human affairs and endeavours, and, like Mercury, is "the inventor of all arts, the guide for every road and journey ... [with] the greatest influence for all money-making and traffic".[68] Like the other Bear Son figures, such as Arthur and Beowulf, Artaois is a strong but wise warrior who knows when to fight and when to withdraw. However, his association with Gwydion reminds us of that he also has powerful magical, possibly shamanic, qualities, although he may sometimes use that magic in mischievous ways. He is Ursa Minor, the Little Bear, looking down from the pole star. Within the three realms he drives on our dreams and achievements from the stars, bringing us success in the apparent world and, from the underworld, helps us to explore our own subconscious and unconscious minds.

Chapter 4

Artio and Artaois today

This chapter will explore the many manifestations of Artio and Artaois in contemporary media and social cultures, from the global (books and movies) to the local (art and creativity) and the deeply personal (identity). The following also represents part of my personal journey, discovering the God and Goddess in those creations that touched my life and beliefs throughout my pilgrimage. These representations do not always bear the name of Artio and Artaois and are by no means exclusive. You may find other manifestations in your own journeys.

Artio and Artaois on Page and Screen

When a friend found out I was writing a book about Bear Gods they ordered me a very wonderful surprise gift from a second-hand book dealer. It was something that they had read in their childhood and for which they still had a great fondness – *Michael Bond's Book of Bears*. Published in 1971, the book is a compilation of bear stories from around the world, including traditional folk tales and poems alongside pieces by Hilaire Belloc, Leo Tolstoy and Evelyn Waugh. Collated by Michael Bond, his ursine hero Paddington, who has been undergoing something of a renaissance in recent years following two charming films, is obviously present, as are the other big hitters Rupert and Winnie the Pooh. In fact, the 'Holy Trinity' of Paddington, Rupert and Pooh are given pride of place on the back cover of the first edition, their renown clearly sufficient enough to entice browsers to purchase this wonderful collection.

However, they are not alone on the back cover. There is a fourth bear with them, standing upright and carrying what looks like a bagful of goodies. This bear is Mary Plain, the creation of

British author Gwynedd Rae who published 14 books about Mary between 1930 and 1965. Mary is a wonderfully cheeky little bear and far more mischievous than her better-known companions Paddington, Rupert and Pooh. However, like the others, Mary has catchphrases and a look of her own. As she puts it "I am Mary Plain, an unusual first-class bear with a white rosette and a gold medal with a picture of myself on it".[1] Her tale in *Michael Bond's Book of Bears* tells how she goes to a birthday party where she gets punched on the nose after a tiff ("Am I blooding?"[2] she asks her guardian, the Owl Man) before using the incident as an excuse for laying on her back and having strawberry ice-cream ladled into her mouth by the birthday girl's mother. Her wicked sense of humour is revealed as she is carried from the party on a stretcher: when one dismayed partygoer asks if Mary is seriously hurt, she replies dryly "Yes. I'm dead".[3]

What makes Mary so special to our investigation is where she comes from. Rae draws her heroine from the bear pits in Bern where this journey began. So, is she a representative of Artio? No, clearly not! Mary Plain is a naughty but charismatic child who mispronounces words and cause chaos. And yet there are features of her character which are important. For a start, she is a girl. The other big hitters of children's bear fiction are all boys and it is really pleasing to find a female character who is cheekier and more rambunctious than their male counterparts. She has a wildness that is oddly missing from Paddington, Rupert, and Pooh. Similarly, like the comparison of Artaois with Gwydion, it is sometimes useful to imagine our Bear Gods as tricksters or, in this case, as capable of being naughty! Sometimes our pursuit of spirituality can be somewhat humourless and we don't see that there is a charming naughtiness in nature. In February 2020 a story spread across social media of three bear cubs photographed in a Finnish forest that appeared to be dancing with each other. Valtteri Mulkahainen, who took the photos described the cubs as "behaving like little children" that "walked on their hind legs, climbed trees and tried to push each other over"[4] before beginning their 'dance'. Mary Plain captures the spirit of these boisterous little cubs and reminds us not to ignore the playful element of nature.

While Mary Plain may have been somewhat forgotten, in terms of young people's fiction there is a new bear in town: Iorek Byrnison. The creation of Philip Pullman, Byrnison appears in several parts of the *His Dark Materials* trilogy, published between 1995 and 2000. He is one of the Panserbjørn, a race of intelligent white bears who wear armour. The protagonist, Lyra Belacqua, first meets Byrnison in a yard behind a bar where he is employed by humans to "mend broken machinery and articles of iron"[5], jobs beneath such a noble creature. The reader soon finds out the Byrnison is being held as punishment in Trollesund for killing two men:

I stay here and drink spirits because the men here took my armour away, and without that, I can hunt seals but I can't go to war; and I am an armoured bear: war is the sea I swim in and the air I breathe.[6]

For Byrnison, the armour is more than just a means to go to war; it is part of him. In Pullman's universe, humans are accompanied by a dæmon, a manifestation of their inner-being which appears in the form of an animal. Byrnison tells Lyra that his armour, which he made for himself, fulfils the same role: "My armour is made of sky-iron, made for me. A bear's armour is his soul, just as your dæmon is your soul".[7] And it is Byrnison's skills with metal which make him of interest in our search for Artaois. Reading *His Dark Materials*, I was reminded of Marie-Louise Sjoestedt assertion that a tribal god like Artaois would be considered "father, nurturer, protector of the tribe, warrior, magician and", most importantly here, "craftsman".[8]

Byrnison's skill as a craftsman is central to the narrative

of *His Dark Materials*. After his rampage in Trollesund "The only reason [the residents] didn't shoot to kill him is because of his wondrous skill with metals"[9] while, in the third book in the trilogy, Lyra announces to her partner that "Oh, he can do anything with metal, Will! Not only armour – he can make little delicate things as well".[10] Pullman vividly shows him leading the complex process of re-forging of the Subtle Knife with Will and Lyra. Perhaps it is because bears have enormous paws that we don't generally associate them with craftsmanship, although a recent study by Washington State University found that Grizzly Bears were able to use rudimentary tools, showing they had "problem-solving and cognitive-thinking skills".[11] Pullman's association of bears with metal working provides us with another interesting aspect to consider for our Bear God, again perhaps resonating through his association with Mercury, "the inventor of all arts".[12]

Byrnison's proficiency and close association with sky-iron, a type of metal found in meteorites, not only connects him with Mercury but also links him back to the realm of the sky and stars. Another connection to Artaois lies in Byrnison's position as a king in exile. This could perhaps be read as a period of hibernation or a descent into the underworld. Pullman gives Byrnison an interesting backstory where he kills another bear in combat over a mate:

> The male Iorek killed would not display the usual signs of surrender when it was clear that Iorek was stronger. For all of their pride, bears never fail to recognize superior force in another bear and surrender to it, but for some reason this bear didn't do it… At any rate, the younger bear persisted, and Iorek Byrnison allowed his temper to master him. The case was not hard to judge; he should have wounded not killed.[13]

Exiled, tricked and sedated with alcohol, Byrnison regains his crown and his heroic self though his adventures with Lyra; he is a literal embodiment of the Bear-Son archetype.

Finally, in this section on Literature, I want to consider the character of Beorn in Tolkien's *The Hobbit*. In Old English, Beorn means "Man; noble, hero, chief, prince, warrior"[14] although there are obvious echoes of the name Beowulf (the "Beo", or bee, element of the name finding physical manifestation in *The Hobbit* with the giant bees which surround Beorn's hall). His name also is cognate for the Scandinavian name Bjorn, meaning bear and, in early drafts of *The Hobbit*, Beorn was named Medwed, with echoes of Medved, the Russian word for bear.[15] Beorn is not a simply a bear. Gandalf describes him as "a skin-changer. He changes his skin; sometimes he is a huge black bear, sometimes he is a great strong black-haired man with huge arms and a great beard".[16] It is Beorn's ability to change between man and bear which makes him interesting for our consideration of Artaois. As a character, he takes us back to the ancient story of the Bear Mother and her Bear Husband, which explores the primal connection between man and bear. Tolkien explores this further as Gandalf considers Beorn's heritage:

> Some say that he is a bear descended from the great and ancient bears of the mountains that lived there before the giants came. Others say that he is a man descended from the first men who lived before Smaug ...[17]

Tolkien presents us with a character who can alternate between being in the shape of a man or a bear, much like the Bear Husband and his kin. In terms of our exploration of Artaois this is important: this shape shifting element is embedded deep in the ancient bear lore.

Tolkien's Beorn is a formidable but a far less sinister presence than his representation in Peter Jackson's film trilogy of *The Hobbit*. In the second movie, *The Desolation of Smaug*, Jackson initially presents Beorn in his bear form, hunting down and chasing Bilbo Baggins and his companions until they have to take refuge in his home. He is not shown in his human form, played by Mikael Persbrandt, until the following morning, when a tense breakfast ensues. In the novel, although anti-social ("He never invited people into his house"[18]), Beorn proves a good host. Tolkien has the character being gently tricked by Gandalf into allowing the travellers into his home and, the following morning at breakfast, Beorn "seemed to be in a splendidly good humour and set them all laughing with his funny stories".[19] This difference carries through to the end of the tale; in *The Battle of the Five Armies*, Jackson keeps Beorn at a distance with him dropping into the conflict but never really getting involved in the main action. In the novel, however, it is Beorn who "stooped and lifted Thorin, who had fallen pierced with spears, and bore him out of the fray"[20] before "he pulled down Bolg [the leader of the Goblin army] himself and crushed him".[21]

However, there is a striking similarity in both the novel and the films – Beorn's closeness to other animals. In the novel, Beorn's home is attended by dogs, ponies and sheep while Beorn also seems to call other bears to talk to him:

"I have been picking up bear tracks," [Gandalf] said at last. "There must have been a regular bear's meeting outside here last night, I soon saw that Beorn could not have made them all: there were far too many of them, and they were of various sizes too. I should say there were little bears, large bears, ordinary bears, and gigantic big bears, all dancing outside from dark to nearly dawn."[22]

To show a similar affinity with the lives in nature, Jackson has Beorn holding a small white mouse as he says "I don't like dwarves. They're greedy and blind, blind to the lives of those they deem lesser than their own". For a moment, it feels like Beorn will crush the mouse which he ultimately gently releases. While Jackson's interpretation is interesting, it is not as developed as Tolkien's. The Beorn of the novel is an interesting, yet pleasing, echo of Artaois: a shape-shifting, anti-social figure, living in a human dwelling but closely connected to the natural world, he ultimately comes to the aid of those who need him.

While many of the bears discussed above have moved from literature to the big screen, there is one twenty first century film which explores the Bear Mother story within a Celtic context and from a fresh angle: Disney Pixar's 2012 movie, *Brave*. Originally titled *The Bear and the Bow*,[23] *Brave* tells the story of Merida, a flame-haired medieval Scottish princess who feels repressed by her mother, Queen Elinor. Seeking a way out, she consults a forest witch, who casts a spell to change her fate and change her mother. The plan backfires badly and her mother is transformed into a bear. As time passes, Elinor begins to becomes "a bear on the inside", slowly losing her humanity.

Central to *Brave* is a contemporary reading of both the Bear Mother myth and the story of Callisto. The Bear Mother story is here explored through the relationship of an overly protective mother and her daughter. Queen Elinor, voiced by Emma Thompson, is absolute in her instructions to Merida about what is and is not appropriate for her to do. At the beginning of the film she is a hectoring annoyance, telling Merida "We can't just run away from who we are", although she focuses more on Merida's royal position than on her personality. Although she is a protective mother, she is everything Artio is not. Elinor acts out of love, but her concerns are misguided and stifle her daughter, rather than letting her blossom. As such, the film works as a contemporary re-focussing of the Bear Mother story, telling the story of a mother who is turned into a bear rather than deeply interrogating the original myth. Even the tale of the Bear Son gets a passing nod, with Elinor and King Fergus' three naughty sons being turned into cheeky bear cubs. The echo of the story of Callisto is perhaps more pertinent. At her angriest, Merida screams "You're a beast" at her mother, her resulting revenge turning the Queen into a form which "is seen as the fallen, bestial side"[24] of Elinor, just as the She-Bear represents a similar bestial side of Callisto. While the movie seems to play fast and loose with these ancient tales, acknowledging them but not really exploring them, the power of old stories lies at the heart of the film. "Legends are lessons" Elinor tells her daughter "they ring with truth". When she hears her daughter repeat her words later in the film, the Queen finally releases her daughter from the weight of tradition and appreciates her for who she really is. What is particularly refreshing is to see these elements within a Celtic setting. The film has some stunning bear imagery, from the wood carvings in the witch's hut, to a bear-headed carnyx and the beautiful bear Celtic knot design of the royal family seen both behind the throne and on Merida's locket.

Although, at various points, the film suggests its central themes are fate and pride, it is about something far more potent, something which leads us back to Artio. It is a film about embracing our own wildness, and what happens if we have too much or not enough wildness in our lives. This is particularly shown through the characterisation of the Queen. When Elinor is initially turned into a bear, she stumbles around the castle, destroying various rooms in her new clumsy and uncoordinated body. However, she insists on placing her delicate golden crown on her enormous, furry head before she and her daughter run into the forest. The next morning, when Merida awakes in the open air and next to a rolling stream, Elinor, still in her bear form, has set a delicate breakfast table and proceeds to try to eat blueberries with a wooden knife and fork. The scene is absurd but wonderful. Merida points out that her mother has actually collected poisonous berries before setting about getting fresh salmon from the river. Even this turns Elinor's stomach as the salmon wriggles, freshly skewered on an arrow. As the scene progresses, Elinor is forced to embrace her bear form, stumbling into the river to comedically grapple with more fish before becoming an adept fisher, plucking salmon out of the air as they leap the waterfall. The bear and her daughter reconnect with each other in the stream, each comfortable in their own skin as the song *Into the Open Air* is sung. While this section does play into the wider narrative about bucking tradition, played out in the beautiful fast flowing river with one character in the figure of the bear, the film seems to be encouraging us to get out into the wilderness and become wild ourselves to find out who we are. However, while a touch of wildness may be healing, the film also warns us about giving into our wild side too much. At several points while she is in bear-form Elinor loses herself completely, her transformation into a bear becoming mental as well as physical, to the point where she begins to attack her daughter. It turns out that that being half-bear and half-human is the perfect balance, just like the ancient myths told us!

For the main antagonist of *Brave*, writer Brenda Chapman created a whole new myth; *The Legend of Mor'du*. While part of the movie, the story of Mor'du was expanded into a short film and was made available on the DVD and Blu-ray release of *Brave*. Mor'du is referred to in *Brave* as "the demon bear". It becomes clear that Mor'du was similarly cursed to take bear form and his transformation into a terrifying and uncontrollable force acts as a warning of what will happen to Elinor if the enchantment is not lifted in time. In the final confrontation, Mor'du is crushed by a standing stone. His human spirit finally released. He smiles at the princess before transforming into one of the friendly will-o'-the-wisps who had helped Merida throughout the film. Here again in Mor'du, the bear represents the most bestial, destructive aspects of humanity.

While all of the texts and films considered so far in this chapter give us echoes of the Bear Gods, there is one realm where Artio is named and presented in both her human and bear form: the online game *Smite*. As its name suggests, *Smite* is a battle arena video game where players assemble groups of Gods and Goddesses from different pantheons to fight each other. The design for Artio is stunning. In her human form she is presented as a red-haired warrior swathed in green Celtic fabric and blue tartan, held together with a bear's head brooch. She has armour around her wrists and waist and carries a staff with a crescent moon shaped axe head at the top. Her bear form is truly intimidating: green glowing eyes mark the creature out as a supernatural being while long plats flow from her head and powerful wrist armour sits around her formidable paws.

While it would be easy to dismiss this Artio as little more than a cypher in a battle game, the background lore given to the character is intricate and thoughtful:

Ice melts in cascading waterfalls from jagged mountain peaks, pouring into rivers roaring white to the cold sea. Straightening slowly, like aged men, trees and fauna of the underbrush, now free of snow-weight, reach for the sun. It is spring; the world awakens from darkness and death to grow green again. Her hibernation ends. Coat wet with fresh rain, Artio, Goddess-Bear, roars into the chill morning air.

She is guardian of the cycle. Not the passage of time, but the balance of things. There is no spring without winter, no death without life, no darkness without light, no goodness without evil. Nature declares these opposites into law and Artio is the enforcer.

Among the ursine she runs, sometimes in the shape of a woman, lithe and wild, sometimes as a bear, brown and fierce. Nowhere in the forest do there stand shrines in her name, for Artio is less worshipped and more respected. Perhaps, instead, she looms overhead, a constant presence in the twinkle of the stars, a connection of glistening light; the constellation Ursa Major.[25]

On the official reveal video for the character, the above text is read over a beautiful animation which feels like an incredibly appropriate introduction to the actual goddess rather than just the game character. In terms of her abilities in the game, Artio can shapeshift between her Druid and Bear form, having different abilities depending on which form she has taken. In her Druid, human form she can decompose her enemy's armour and create a web of entangling vines to pin them to the ground. She can also rip out her enemy's life force while they are stuck. In her bear form, she can let out a ferocious roar which stuns her enemy and then undertake a heavy charge before mauling them. In the God reveal video she is described as a "bruiser",[26] and the online game play certainly shows that she would be a useful character to have on a team! In her God Announcement video, Artio is heard to say "winning or losing doesn't matter. We all shall return to nature in the end".[27] Deeply connected to nature and Celtic lore, *Smite's* Artio is a potent avatar of the Goddess for the gaming generation.

And He was Made of Stars

Having explored texts such as films and books, I would like to explore a manifestation of Artaois I discovered while in Glastonbury at the end of 2019. I found myself being drawn to several pieces of work by the same artist: Hannah Willow. Hannah is an artist and jewellery maker from Wiltshire whose work reflects the British landscape and wildlife. I initially noticed many beautiful representations of badgers and hares in her work but, as I browsed, I found a piece called *Going Home for Winter* with a sleepy brown bear trudging through a snowy forest. At first, I was slightly taken aback. After all, Hannah's work is so focused around British wildlife that to find a bear in the middle of the hares, stags, and badgers was something of a surprise. But then I found a piece which truly took my breath away.

Deep in the autumnal woodland, a badger sits amongst ferns and grasses looking up at a silvery, opaque figure before him. It is the figure of a bear, standing on its hind paws looking down beneficently on the badger at his feet. Trails of light and stars emanate from the bear, weaving through the woodland and out into the night sky, where the constellation of Ursa Major runs beneath the moon. A chalk White Horse glints in the moonlight. The bear's coat shimmers with star dust, a small crescent moon hangs among the hairs. The title of this piece of work is *And He was Made of Stars*.

Enthused by the sight of a bear standing so solidly in a clearly British landscape, I contacted Hannah to see if she could tell me more about her work and, particularly about the iconography of *And He was Made of Stars*. I started by asking her where her inspiration came from: "I get my inspiration from mythology, folklore and the landscape of the British Isles", she told me. "I'm also inspired by prose and poetry, in particular the work of Thomas Traherne, Mary Oliver, Wendell Berry and others". I went on to ask her why she worked with the image of the bear when it is no longer in the British landscape. She reasoned "I am very interested in Bears and what they represent to us emotionally and spiritually. In my work they bring an aspect of both universal and earthly wisdom. They are fiercely protective of the Earth and the animals living here and they bring an ancestral knowledge and energy to the work." I went back to the question I had asked others previously, which had been so central to my search for Artio and Artaois: did Hannah still feel the bear was a part of the British Landscape? "Yes, I do, particularly in the energetic similarity between bears and badgers. I feel that the bear is badly needed back in our landscape, even if only within our hearts and our imaginations."

This connection between bears and badgers is not new, but Hannah's work seems to express it in particularly vivid terms for me. The badger, in *And He was Made of Stars* looks up at the figure in front of him as if he were greeting a distant cousin, welcoming him back with real warmth and affection. I asked Hannah how she perceived the relationship between bears and badgers more generally: "Well, on a purely personal level they feel very similar energetically, earthy creatures that inhabit the dark places in woodlands and within the landscape. They look very cuddly but are in fact quite the opposite. And so, for me, they hold the balance of beauty and grace, but also a fierce presence that needs our deep respect."

Before I told her how much I loved *And He was Made of Stars*, I asked Hannah if she had her own favourite amongst her bear pieces and was not surprised when she told me it was the same picture. I asked her why she liked it so much: "I like the relationship between the earthly Badger and the ethereal Bear, the wonder in the heart of the badger as he sees the Star-Bear and wonders why he has appeared." I asked if there was a particular inspiration for the piece: "I was thinking of Badgers as protectors of the earth, and how similar bears are to them. I imagined an ancestor bear returning to appear to a badger, to remind him of his role in the landscape and show that he was loved and supported through time eternal."

As the connection between bears and stars was so strong in her work, I asked Hannah if it is a motif she has used elsewhere. "I love to incorporate the Bear star constellations in my bear pictures if I can" she told me "and also in my silver work too. I'm interested in the ancient peoples seeing animals, birds, gods and goddesses in the stars and naming the patterns they saw. For me, the Bear constellations are protective, overseers of the earth as she travels through space, looking down and observing the land." As she had raised the connection between animals, gods and stars, I asked Hannah if she had heard of Artio and Artaois. "I haven't", she told me "but I will be researching them now!"

To finish our interview, I asked Hannah if she had any future plans for including bears in her work and was thrilled by her response. "Yes, I do have plans for more Bear images, and also plans for a short book with the two characters from *And He was Made of Stars*. Hopefully, I will get time to illustrate it!" I love the idea of a book based around this beautiful, evocative image and can't wait to see how the story develops. Hannah's work with bears may not be directly inspired by Artio and Artaois, but the protective, earthy energy she portrays in them clearly link them to their Celtic ancestors. Copies of Hannah's work, including *And He was made of Stars* can be found at her website, www.hannahwillow.com.

The Goddess and the Gay Bear Scene

As a gay man, one of the questions I asked myself during my early experiences with Artio was whether I was being led to this Goddess because of my sexuality. In the sense of gay culture and sub-cultures, I would be classified as a 'bear', someone who is of larger build and somewhat hairy. The Bear scene began in California in the 1960s with groups and clubs beginning to be set up in the UK from the late 1980s. Much work has been done on charting the history, aesthetics and values of Bear culture, from the engagingly accessible articles like *A Brief History of the Gay Bears and Big Boys Scene*,[28] to more analytical work such as *The Bear Book* edited by Les Wright. Wright states that:

Since the term "bear" is applied in a self-defining manner, it is vaguely defined, sometimes in self-contradictory ways, and is interpreted variously. Human identification with totemic, symbolic, and physical attributes of bears has a long history and plays a key role in the specifically gay male adoption of the term. It may describe physical size, refer to male secondary sex characteristics, to alleged behaviours or personality traits of bears, or to metaphysical, supernatural, or other symbolic attributes of bears. Thus, it is impossible to answer the question "What is a bear?" in any definitive way, beyond the array of connotative associations in our culture...[29]

I wondered if these "connotative associations" might lead me to find some echoes of the Celtic Bear Gods within Gay Bear culture. Having not really explored the scene much myself, I asked my friend and fellow OBOD member Ricky Gellissen about his spiritual experiences as someone who had been involved in the Bear scene in the UK from its early days.

I found that we had similar experiences in terms of exploring the connection between sexuality and bear iconography: "If memory serves correctly, I was aware of Artio before but starting seeing her as a principal deity in 2012 after re-examining my relationship with Bears on an OBOD course about meditation and ritual. I had been averse to embracing bears as any form of spirit guide, or forging too close an affiliation with a bear deity, as it did seem too stereotypically gay to declare 'I'm a bear and all things bear are thus sacred to me'. I specifically avoided donning bearskin in a skin walking meditation exercise, opting instead for raccoon (Der Waschbär: literally, "wash-bear" or "washing bear"). Discussion both with other course participants, course tutors and, later, my OBOD mentor led me to stop the aversion of falling to stereotype and embracing what connections might naturally be there." I asked Ricky what it was about Artio that really appealed to him: "I like the 'Schrödinger's Bear' issue of the Deae Artioni sculpture: that the statue depicts either the Goddess facing a bear or the bear facing a supplicant. So little is known that I like allowing the flexibility of deity in my mind." Interestingly, when asked about Artois, Ricky stated that he had no sense of a male bear deity or a male form of Artio.

I went on to ask Ricky if he had ever encountered any sense of the Celtic Bear Gods within Bear culture. "As the Bear Scene came across from the USA," he told me "I found that most of the iconography in any spiritual sense was borrowed from First Nation Americans rather than connecting with mythology or spirituality outside of North America." When I questioned him further about the link between Artio and the current Bear scene he replied "I doubt many are aware of Artio and, because it is becoming more and more hyper-masculinised, I doubt that many would embrace a Bear Goddess. Obviously, I know of some gay pagans who aware of the Bear Goddess and have entered ritual space with two other Bears who follow Druidry and affiliate to Artio, but I cannot think of many specifically Pagan Bears I know who speak of her."

I asked Ricky more about his spiritual work with the two friends he had mentioned and how Artio was present in their ceremonies: "Between the three of us, as all are in the same seedgroup which is much larger than us and is not specifically LGBTQ+ but has many LGBTQ+ members, I think Artio has been welcomed into our circle at most rituals and celebrations. In any ceremony, acknowledging Bear as a representation of the element of Earth and a spirit of the North, Artio is always there." Ricky also mentioned that they had developed two festivals specifically designed to honour Artio: The Feasts of Artio Rising and Artio Retiring. "We first held an event in 2016 when we decided to acknowledge the syncretism of Artio and St. Ursula, to mark a day of honour for her. Some believe Artio was absorbed into Christianity as the British Saint Ursula ('Little Female Bear'), a Latinized form of the Saxon 'Ursel' meaning 'She Bear'. Her feast day is October 21 which provided an interesting parallel with the harvest attribute seen on the statue of Artio in Bern. This seemed as good a day as any to dedicate to her and became the Feast of Artio Retiring. Looking at the Deae Artioni statue, I had a discussion with one of my friends, Ferdiad, where he suggested the woman was feeding the Goddess in her form as a bear rather than the human figure being the Goddess. We could see both the images of the bear and the image of the human as being Artio. We realised that the dual representation could be used to dedicate a day to her at both Autumn and Spring. As Artio is a bear then there is a perceived link to fertility and fruition, since breeding bears spend their hibernation pregnant and give birth when they rise in the spring. So, St. Ursula's Day would be pre-hibernation, and could be associated with harvest, with preparing for Winter and the journey into darkness. We then decided there could be a second day around early Spring to mark the emergence from hibernation, the new cubs, the return to the light, and any wisdom/transformation from the journey. So, alongside the Feast of Artio Retiring in October we designated the first new moon after Imbolc as the Feast of Artio Rising." Ricky's suggestions here very much tie in with the suggested dates to celebrate Artio as seen in Chapter 3. However, the benefit of having two feasts, honouring both the sense of harvest and the sense of emergence from the Underworld, addresses the complex nature of Artio's role.

After my discussion with Ricky, I could not really find any connection between Artio, Artaois and the wider Bear Scene. However, I feel that the work of Ricky and his fellow Bear Druids is really important. By acknowledging and moving beyond the stereotypical association of gay men and Bear Gods, they have been able to connect with the essence of the Goddess herself. The Feasts of Artio Rising in February and Artio Retiring in October reconcile the traditions of the Celtic Brigid and Swedish St Birgitta as mentioned in the previous chapter, and give those who follow the Bear-Goddess two opportunities to acknowledge her many aspects and attributes. I also found Ricky's earlier comment on how the Bear Scene has become hypermasculine very interesting. Now that there is more emphasis on muscles and masculinity, perhaps Artaois, the incarnation of the Bear Son and precursor to our modern heroes, may become more of a totem for the Bear community.

The Bear Tribe

While we were chatting about Ricky's work with Artio, he told me that he had "also explored Arctolatry joining members of The Bear Tribe on the Mid-Winter Bear Feast." Intrigued as to the activities of this Bear Tribe, I investigated further and got in touch with Corwen Broch who established the movement with Kate Fletcher. What Kate and Corwen have created is extraordinary. Using the research in Hallowell's *Bear Ceremonialism in the Northern Hemisphere*, they have established a framework for a recreation of the ancient Bear Feast. They have also held several Bear Feasts at Cranborne Ancient Technology Centre with their work inspiring groups around the world.

I asked Corwen where the initial ideas for this event came from and he told me "Before we were married, my wife Kate and I were walking the pilgrimage to Santiago de Compostela in 2005. We had a lot of time to talk, including about religion. We discussed the ideas I had heard from Graham Harvey during a talk he gave at a Druid camp some years earlier. He discussed how one of the origins of religion was the need for people to make amends for killing plants and animals for food, or keep good relations with the beings, spirits, or gods that 'own' those animals and plants. We also discussed the origins of religion and the Bear Cult being a candidate for the world's oldest religion. The link between these two strands of our conversation was obvious. Crossing the Pyrenees on the summer solstice it came together with the idea to revive the Bear Feast with the explicit idea of exploring ideas of our relationship with food and the necessary killing, upon which our lives depend." I am particularly interested in this link between the ancient Bear Feast and its utilisation by Kate and Corwen as a way of considering all of the food we eat. After all, Artio's role as a Goddess of the harvest clearly links with this sense of appreciating the source of all of the food we have eaten. "Bear Feast is the ritual of a mystery religion," Corwen told me, "a sacred meal and communion which attempts to explore artistically and spiritually one of the questions of life; that life is precious, yet depends on death to continue, the death of those who are in reality our kin."

"The connection between most people in the West and nature is extremely tenuous. Likewise, our appreciation of the reality of the lives and deaths of the other-than-human-persons we depend upon for food is similarly tenuous. We collectively have a slim grasp on these realities, and work hard to keep it that way. Our culture has a couple of conflicting ideas about this written into it and, even though these ideas conflict on the surface, they work together to shut out feelings of responsibility and compassion towards other-than-human-persons. One such idea is that God gave human beings unique power over the non-human world to exploit as we wish, and the corollary is that humans are thus in some way special and unique in our consciousness or souls. We aren't. Secondly is the idea that nothing has a soul; all living things are just mechanisms and that nothing therefore has any intrinsic value or rights. Of course, this second idea also erodes the value of humans too, but we gloss over that by telling ourselves how unique our form of consciousness is in a variation of the first story. Both stories are of course nonsense. The hard fact is that those animals and plants we kill to eat are conscious beings with personhood like ours. It is a hard fact, but one that, if we embrace it, gives our lives tremendous value and meaning as we accept that our continued existence means the end of the existence of others. We can choose to meet this reality head on and do what we can to show gratitude to those other beings and the wider world, the effect of which is to give value to both our lives and the lives of those other beings."

He clarified "We do not have any particular agenda with Bear Feast; we are not preaching vegetarianism, meat eating, veganism or anything else but Bear Feast exists as a way of expressing our gratitude for life and exploring what we feel about these issues."

I asked Corwen to outline a typical Bear Feast event. "The

feast begins with a time of community bonding first, eating together and learning the songs we'll use in the ritual. The next morning, we have the hunt, which is book-ended with ritual to protect the hunters. This both creates a sense of shared sacred space and gives thanks to the Bear for giving him or herself so that we might eat. In the hunt, a person impersonates the Bear and is killed by the hunters in the way dictated by circum-polar traditions. The hunters then ceremonially remove the Bear skin from the person wearing it. The Bear is brought into the ritually prepared space and coins are placed on the eyes of the Bear skin to signify that he is present. As part of that we have games and performances to honour the Bear who is a guest at the meal where he is, symbolically in our case, also the food."

"The Bear acts as a sort of substitute for, or psychopomp of, all the lives we have necessarily taken through our continued existence in the previous year. There is a meditation to bring this idea to the fore. Then there is a sacred meal. After that, more performances, particularly songs and poetry, and finally the 'soul' of the Bear is sent back to his origin, the Sky Father, taking with him messages of thanks. This has been done by placing the skull in a pine tree, by hoisting him out of the hole in a roundhouse roof, and a couple of other ways over the years depending on where the ritual has been held. Sometimes we have let off a firework as a sign of his ascent. It marks the end of the sacred part of the ritual. Even though I am a rational person and don't believe in souls or spirits, the sense of the presence of the Bear, and then its absence, is palpable."

I asked Corwen how many Bear Feasts had been held: "There have been nine big Bear Feasts with many people attending. There have been a fair number of other smaller Feasts held in people's houses and woodlands, and even one which held the hunt part in in a public park. Many other people who have attended one or more feasts celebrate in their homes with a sacred meal and perhaps by singing the songs rather than carry out the full ritual." And it isn't only in Britain that Kate and Corwen's work is being used to bring the Bear Feasts back; the work has taken on a life of its own: "There have been Feasts in the USA and in the Basque country as well as the UK. The Manual is on the internet free to download so it may have happened elsewhere without our knowledge."

As Corwen mentioned, a copy of instruction manual for carrying out your own Bear Feast is available from www. beartribe.co.uk. The manual is incredibly comprehensive and includes full instructions for how to run a Bear Feast and who should be involved. As Kate and Corwen work with ancient music played on ancient instruments, a full set of songs and chants is included, drawn from many different sources. "Most of the words in this ritual are recorded oral utterances of people from around the sub-arctic world. As oral poetry, fixed in time when it was recorded, it was never meant to be a final or permanent version, but a performance alive in its moment. With this in mind, participants are free to paraphrase, rewrite, misremember and change the words to suit themselves!" There is also a list of games to be played in honour of the slain bear, from traditional axe and spear throwing, to the more irreverent Sprout Flinging with Slingshots! "Most of the games have a food theme; since Bear Feast is about food this makes sense. Vegetable related sport is a sort of running joke too in our lives! Please ensure at least one of your games involves Brussel Sprouts or the Great God Brassica may be offended!"

The Bear Feast is intended to be run over three days in the depths of winter: "We used to hold the ritual on the Winter Solstice. A good time would be the 'navel of winter', or Talvennapa in Finnish, which is three weeks after the Solstice in mid-January." However, if you cannot commit to a three-day ritual, the manual also gives instructions for how to run an event in one day or even an evening, as well as ways of honouring the festival known as Karhunpäivä. "This is a particularly

Finnish and Estonian tradition rather than being circum-polar. Karhunpäivä is the Bear's birthday, it is celebrated opposite to Talvennapa, in the 'navel of summer', on the 13th July. We take our lead from the Finnish Arctolatrist organisation Karhun Kansa for this ritual, who have spent much time researching it. We try to wear white if we can, we abstain from going into the woods as a way of giving nature some space away from us humans for the day. We also make promises about what we will do to help nature in the coming year, witnessed by the presence of our Bear skull. We also sing the Origin song of the Bear taken from *The Kalevala*".

While it is clear that Kate and Corwen have put an enormous amount of time and thought into the manual and the events, they encourage other to experiment with the form: "The suggestions given in the manual are not meant to be slavishly followed. They do not represent any attempt at describing the best way to do anything, it just describes how we have done things before. We encourage people to use their imagination and common sense."

The resurrection of this primal festival, while not having any specific link to the Celtic Bear Gods Artio and Artaois, does link us back to what Corwen calls "One of Mankind's oldest spiritual impulses: Arctolatry, the Worship of the Bear." As this chapter has shown, the echoes of Artio and Artaois in modern society do not always bear their names, although they can lead us to a deeper understanding of their roles. The Bear Feast is a connection back to the early story of the Bear Mother and her Husband who sacrificed himself for the good of the tribe and, in this sense, does link us to the foundations of who Artio may have been and how those who worshiped her honoured her. By exploring the form of the ancient Bear Feast with a sense of being thankful for all of the food we consume, I personally feel that Corwen and Kate's ritual works incredibly well in directly honouring Artio, the vegetation Goddess and provider of the harvest. The dual aspect of the statue in Bern, where Artio resides in both the human and bear figures, both presenting and receiving the harvest, is echoed in the heart of the Bear Feast where life is acknowledged as being deeply precious, yet dependent on the death of others to continue. Similarly, this leads us again to Artio's role as not only purveyor of the harvest but also the protective mother who leads us into the underworld at our death.

There may also be a sense of the roots of Artaois, the questing Bear Son, within the Bear Feast. The connection between Artaois and his counterpart Arthur is something Corwen believes may be at the heart of this ritual: "In Arthurian myth, Arthur, like a hibernating Bear, sleeps until he is needed, his grail or cauldron feeds all comers and like the Bear in the circumpolar traditions this cauldron descends from heaven on a chain. These elements of Arthurian myth sound to me like a garbled remembering of the original Bear Feast, with its sacred meal and sleeping King." If T.W. Rolleston's proposal is right, and elements of Artaois mixed with the emerging tale of Arthur, then perhaps we can begin to see some elements of his worship in this resurrected ancient ritual.

The work of the Bear Tribe is the perfect end point for my journey through time and place to piece together the nature and traditions surrounding Artio and Artaois. It takes us back to the earliest human rituals and asserts their relevance again in the twenty first century. It reminds us that the sense of thankfulness and reverence our ancestors acknowledged in their ritual is still relevant today. At a time of ecological peril, the re-emergence of iconography and ritual associated with the bear gods, humanity's primal animal totem, should be of great significance and comfort for those who walk the path of nature religions. They show us that our original Mother and her son have not left us. They have merely been sleeping and are waking up again to guide us.

Chapter Five

Honouring Artio and Artaois

After my journeys and discoveries, I want to consider ways that we can honour Artio and Artaois in our everyday life. Depending on your relationship with the Bear Gods you may want to undertake a small act of devotion or something much bigger.

Prayer and Devotion

While uttering short, impromptu prayers is a good way to communicate with Artio and Artaois, there is a joy in crafting something more thoughtful and structured. By spending time working through how you want to address the Bear Gods, you can make your prayer more personal. While writing, remember that these pieces of work are meant to be spoken aloud, so read them out regularly to ensure that you are able to articulate them fully.

Writing and speaking your own words as prayer is a powerful thing to do and you may find that you learn the piece by heart and speak it aloud again and again. Many faiths have such standard prayers which are uttered regularly and which followers know and speak together. There are several ways of viewing such prayers: you may find that saying the same words repeatedly brings the comfort of tradition. Conversely, you may find sticking to the same prayer format restrictive or suffocating. Wherever you stand on this, spending time writing one or a number of different prayers for the Bear Gods helps you to really focus on who they are and how you can work with them.

In terms of what to include in your prayers, you may want to use some words and phrases found in this book, perhaps adapting the Romano-Celtic inscriptions to "Dea Artio" or using some of the synonyms used by the many circum-polar Bear Feasts (examples of which can be found in Chapter 3 and later in this chapter).

One final thing to consider. While prayer is positive, I always like to follow it up with practical action. Perhaps as part of your devotion you could donate to a bear charity or sponsor a rescued bear. While working with bears may seem like the most direct way to honour Artio and Artaois, it is not the only way you can devote yourself to them. Donating or working with your local Food Bank, ensuring those in need have enough to eat, for example, is a wonderful way of honouring Artio, the goddess of harvest and plenty.

Creating an Altar

An altar is a beautiful way of honouring a deity, either permanently or as part of a seasonal cycle. Although my altar is more general, I have different bears that stay on the altar all year round, including the Solstice Bear created by Beth Wildwood, as mentioned in Chapter 1. I also have a small pewter bear which I bought from the museum in Bern, who sparkles amongst the rocks and stones in the centre. However, perhaps the most important bear on my altar is a beautiful clay statue, which has very personal resonances. It is the story behind the statue which makes it important for me rather than the statue itself and I think it is that personal engagement with items which is key to creating any altar. You could buy all sorts of bear paraphernalia to decorate the space, but I feel an artefact should tug on your heart or stimulate your senses every time you look at it. Try picking things which really mean something to you and make them sacred by devoting them to the Bear Gods. Reusing items also helps to reduce waste and stop over production, which is appropriate when working with Gods so deeply connected to the Earth.

The Bear Wheel of the Year

While I was exploring the Temple of Ursa with Louisa Potter I found that she has created a Wheel of the Year for her Bear Oracle work (more information can be obtained by Louisa at www.bearfootwalkingtempleofursa.com). As someone very keen on working with the Wheel of the Year, I thought that I would create something similar as a way of honouring Artio and Artaois.

At first, I split the focus of the festivals between the two deities, so that they had four corresponding festivals each, although when I reviewed this the division seemed to be quite arbitrary. I decided to simply look at each festival for what it was and match it on to the bear lifecycle. While I did end up with some festivals specifically for Artaois at the solstices, I wanted to balance this out with festivals specifically for Artio too. These ended up being at Samhain and Imbolc, rather like the Feasts of Artio Retiring and Rising discussed with Ricky. The others ended up being joint festivals where both deities were very much celebrated together. An outline of the Wheel of the Year is included below:

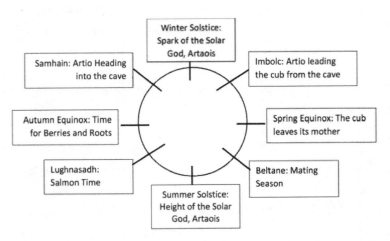

Beginning with Winter Solstice, this festival seemed to fit many of the new life festivals found at this time of year, although brown bears tend to have their cubs later, between January and March. Here I have named it the "Spark of the Solar God", the ignition of the flame of hope in the darkness. This seemed to lead nicely into the ideas of emergence from the darkness, the cave, at Imbolc. Traditionally the first stirring of spring and honouring of Brighid, Imbolc celebrates the quickening, so the idea of the mother bear, Artio, leaving the cave with her new cub fitted nicely here. More complex was the Spring Equinox, which I have here labelled as the Cub leaving its mother. In reality, cubs stay with their mother between two to three years, however, that parting of the pair, with the cub setting off to start its new life, seemed appropriate at this point on the Wheel. Obviously, Artaois is the spirit of the new cub at the Spring Equinox but, at the next festival, is manifested as a fully grown adult male bear. Just as Beltane is about fertility, I have focused on mating season for this festival. Again, this is broadly appropriate with Brown Bear behaviour as they mate between early May and July.

At the Summer Solstice, I reverted to focusing purely on Artaois as the embodiment of the Celtic Sun God, worshipping him at his most powerful but also at the point of his decline. The following two festivals, Lughnasadh and the Autumn Equinox traditionally focus on the grain and fruit harvests so here I have marked them as the time of plenty, Salmon Time, and as a time of preparing more carefully for the winter to come, a Time for Roots and Berries. While catching of salmon from rivers is generally associated with Grizzly Bears in North America, it is such an iconic image and such a potent symbol of plenty that it really seemed to suit the spirit of Lughnasadh. By moving on to roots and berries at the Equinox, the festival helps to suggest that the time of plenty is over, that we need to search more closely for nature's bounty. Samhain marks the descent into the underworld. While both male and female bears den for winter, I wanted to make this specific to Artio to form a narrative over the following few festivals with the beginning of denning, the birth of the cub and the emergence from the cave. Of course, it would be appropriate to mark the death of Artaois at this festival with him returning to the otherworld, ready to be reborn as the cub at the Winter Solstice.

As with many of the elements of this book, this Wheel of the Year is purely a suggestion. There is nothing quite as spiritually developing as working through the Wheel of the Year in your own way and finding your own path, writing your own rituals.

Creating specific Feasts and Festivals

In my search to find a day or days to honour Artio and Artaois, I was particularly drawn to the festivals created by Ricky and his friends, those of Artio Rising and Artio Retiring. The Feast of Artio Retiring was suggested as a way of honouring the harvest aspect of Artio's role, as clearly seen on the statue in Bern. The date used by Ricky and his friends is October 21st. Sitting in between the Autumn Equinox and Samhain, a festival on October 21st marks both the completion of the harvest and the point when bears begin denning for the winter. Writing a ceremony to mark this festival should include reflection on harvests in our lives, both physical and spiritual, as well as marking the beginning of a time of reflection and looking inwards.

The Feast of Artio Rising celebrates the emergence of the Goddess and the self from a time of inward reflection and rest, looking forward to the spring and the new life of the Cub. While there are some arguments for celebrating this at Imbolc, Ricky and friends found an interesting solution here, celebrating the Feast of Artio Rising on the full moon after Imbolc. By doing this, they not only preserved the traditional focus Brighid at Imbolc, but also took account of the link between bear-deities and the heavens. At this festival we should focus on the sense of awakening in the world, as spring begins to gather pace, but also of the emergence of the cub from the cave with its mother. For us, the cub can represent our wishes and desires for the following year, something we want to achieve or manifest in our life. We have a chance to 'lick it into shape', to mould our wishes into something more purposeful, just as She-Bears were believed to lick their cubs into shape in the den.

While overwriting the whole Celtic Wheel of the Year gives us a keen focus on both Artio and Artaois, the Feasts of Artio Rising and Retiring have the benefit of adding specific festivals into our spiritual lives. Personally, I love the variety of the Celtic Wheel of the Year, which gives each season a very different feel and focus, so will be augmenting that calendar with these feasts in years to come.

But what about Artaois, is there a time we could celebrate him with a feast of his own? Well, it is possible to celebrate him as a Sun-God, honouring him at the Solstices, as suggested previously, or at other traditional festivals such as Lughnasadh. However, by exploring the link between Artaois and Ursa Minor, it would be interesting to celebrate a Feast of Artaois that connected with that constellation, perhaps tying it in with the Ursid Meteor Shower which generally occurs in the Northern Hemisphere around the Winter Solstice in December. By creating a festival timed with the meteor shower, one could still explore the idea of the return of the light and the return of the sun, perhaps giving it more of a sense of Artaois falling to Earth, like the meteors tumbling through the sky. This would tie in with the sense of the spirit of the bear coming to Earth from the heavens, as seen in so many ancient myths.

Hold your own Bear Feast

One of the other ways you may choose to honour Artio and Artaois is in staging your own version of the Bear Feast. This could be staged on one of the dates suggested above or on Talvennapa, the Finnish 'navel of winter'. Kate Fletcher and Corwen Broch's manual for how to stage a Bear Feast is detailed and authoritative. It is available to download free of charge from their website: www.beartribe.co.uk. There you will also find pictures from previous events, a range of information about Animism and sound clips for many different songs they have created to use as part of your ritual.

Perhaps the most important song in the manual, one which is repeated on a number of occasions, is the *Honeypaw Song*. Based on the ancient circum-polar tradition of not speaking the Bear's real name during the hunt or feast, in case you offend him, the song acts as both a polite invocation and blessing for the honoured guest. The music is simultaneously joyous and haunting, strongly evoking the ancient traditions described by Hallowell. Words and music for *Honeypaw* are reproduced here with kind permission of Kate Fletcher and Corwen Broch:

Big foot, Broadfoot Lightfoot, Sticky-mouth
Short-tail, Bobtail Snubnose, Honeypaw
Wild Dweller, Footstep Widener, Night Time Prowler, Golden Feet x2
Bee Wolf, Forest Apple, Winter Sleeper, Golden Friend x2
Earth Owner, Forest master, Mountain Ruler, Golden King x2

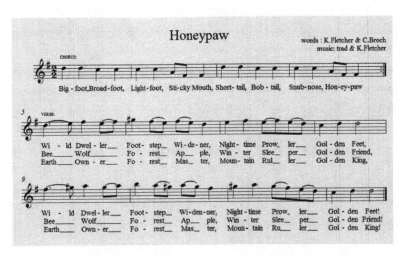

***Honeypaw* by Corwen Broch and Kate Fletcher**

Other songs, such as an accompaniment to the recitation of the *Origins of Otso* from *The Kalevala* are also available for you to download and use.

As mentioned previously, if you aren't able to hold a full, three-day Bear Feast, the manual will give you suggestions for how to develop a ritual for a one day event or even an evening's meal and ritual. Similarly, if you would like to use the work of the Bear Tribe to inspire your own version of the Bear Feast, the manual has an excellent list of suggested reading to help you explore the subject in greater depth. For anyone interested in the Bear Gods, the work of the Bear Tribe is authoritative and inspiring.

Make a Pilgrimage to Bern

Perhaps the most potent way of honouring Artio is to make a pilgrimage to see her statue in Bern. Having made this pilgrimage at the start of my exploration, it is something I can highly recommend. I recognise that it was an incredible privilege for me to be able to make that journey and to experience everything I did in Bern. You may not feel that this experience is available to you but, with careful planning and budgeting, a few days break in Bern is achievable and can really help you connect with the spirit of the Bear-Goddess.

There are a number of practical factors you need to consider when planning your pilgrimage, the most pressing being how you can visit the city whilst doing the least possible damage to the environment. For me, that meant taking the train, however you will need to weigh up the travel options in your part of the world and book your journey accordingly.

In terms of other practicalities, Switzerland is an expensive place to visit and you will need plenty of money for your stay in Bern. For me, it was the food which seemed to be the most expensive, so, if you are planning on eating out, you need to be prepared for those costs. As Switzerland's capital, Bern has a good range of accommodation for different budgets. Personally, I would recommend that you stay in the Old Town which has so much atmosphere. It also gives you the best access to both the Bear Garden and the Historical Museum, as well as having statues, carvings and murals of bears every few steps. The city's website, www.bern.com, has plenty of information including a range of accommodation from hotels to campsites.

The website of the Bern Historical Museum, www.bhm.ch, has up to date information on prices and opening times for you to visit Artio's statue in the 'Stone Age, Celts and Romans' exhibition. Similarly, further information about the Bärenpark, including opening times, can be found at the Bern Animal Park website, www.tierpark-bern.ch, where webcams will also help you to see the bears if you are unable to visit in person.

My time in Bern was incredibly special. I fell in love with the city and the bears. It was deeply spiritual and truly helped me connect to the spirit of Artio. I hope to be able to return one day. It is my sincere wish that you too can make a pilgrimage to this beautiful city at some point in the future.

Afterword

The Onward Path.

The journey outlined in this book has been an incredibly personal experience and I thank you for sharing it with me. I always intended this to be a creative journey towards the Bear Gods. While I have tried to follow the trail of evidence, I acknowledge that, at times, my own personal views may have led me down particular routes. I am neither an anthropologist nor a historian, but an enthusiastic devotee of Artio, so may have missed paths which were more obvious to others. I feel privileged to have had the opportunity to meet so many interesting, passionate and creative individuals along the path. I began with quite a broad understanding of Artio but little real sense of Artaois. While my understanding of both is clearer, I do not feel this journey is at an end. I will continue to both learn about and from Artio and Artaois for the rest of my life.

Although this book is finished, my journey through the forest continues.

"Exit, pursued by a Bear."

Endnotes

Introduction
1   Green (2011), pp 9-10.

Chapter 1
1   Carr-Gomm (2019) p.32.

2   https://balkancelts.wordpress.com/tag/armagh-bear-stat-ues/ (accessed 30.8.19)

3   Green (1992) p.45

4   Green (2011) p.32

5   http://theses.univ-lyon2.fr/documents/getpart. php?id=lyon2.2009.beck_n&part=159143%20 (accessed 26.8.19)

6   Green (1992) p.218

7   https://www.eifel.info/a-schweinestaelle (accessed 26.8.19)

8   http://theses.univ-lyon2.fr/documents/getpart. php?id=lyon2.2009.beck_n&part=159143%20 (accessed 26.8.19)

9   Gimbutas (2001) p.183

10 CIL 13, 7375 [4, p 125] accessed at https://arachne.uni-koeln. de/Tei-Viewer/cgi-bin/teiviewer.php?manifest=BOOK-ZID1318106 (accessed 28.6.19)

11 http://www.arbre-celtique.com/encyclopedie/artio-3413.htm (accessed 26.8.19)

12 http://theses.univ-lyon2.fr/documents/getpart. php?id=lyon2.2009.beck_n&part=159143 (accessed 26.8.19)

13 Gimbutas (2001) p.183

14 Müller (2009) p.258

15 Green (2011) p.189

16 Green (1992) p.218

17 Toynbee (2013) p.99

18 Kaufmann-Heinimann, trans. Dr Eva Funk (2002) p.52.

19 Kaufmann-Heinimann, trans Dr Eva Funk (2002) p.54.

20 Green (2011) p.70

21 Shepherd and Sanders (1985) p.57.

22 Green (1992) p.219

23 Shepherd and Sanders (1985) pp. 75-76.

24 Carr-Gomm, (2005) p.11

25 Green (1992) p.218

26 CIL XII, 2199

27 https://www.revolvy.com/page/Artaius (accessed 8.9.19)

28 Green (2011) p.32

29 Green (2011) P36

30 Sjoestedt (2000) p.15

31 Sjoestedt (2000) p.22

32 De Bell. Gall., vi, 17 (tr Edwards) quoted in Sjoestedt, (2000) p.20.

33 Carr-Gomm (2019) p.31

34 Sjoestedt (2000) p.22

35 Sjoestedt (2000) p.93

36 https://www.druidry.org/library/animals/bear (accessed 9.9.19)

37 Shepherd and Sanders (1985) p.57.

38 Sjoestedt (2000) p.93

39 Sjoestedt (2000) p.93

Chapter 2

1 https://wildplace.org.uk/explore-the-park/bear-wood (accessed 24.09.19)

2 https://wildplace.org.uk/explore-the-park/bear-wood (accessed 24.09.19)

3 https://wildplace.org.uk/explore-the-park/bear-wood (accessed 24.09.19)

4 https://www.theguardian.com/world/2019/jul/19/bear-wood-project-brings-lost-species-back-to-uks-ancient-forests (accessed 24.09.19)

5   O'Regan (2018) p. 230

6   O'Regan (2018) p. 239

7   O'Regan (2018) p. 240

8   O'Regan (2018) p. 240

9   Gary Wills, quoted at https://www.neatorama .com/201 2/01/12/shakespeares-bear/ (accessed 24.09.19)

10   Gary Wills, quoted at https://www.neatorama.com/201 2/01/12/shakespeares-bear/ (accessed 24.09.19)

11   https://www.coventrytelegraph.net/news/revealed-war-wickshires-controversial-bear-ragged-12979079 (accessed 24.09.19)

12   https://apps.warwickshire.gov.uk/api/documents/WCCC-863-86 (accessed 24.09.19)

13   Shepherd and Sanders (1985) p. 128

14   https://apps.warwickshire.gov.uk/api/documents/WCCC-863-86 (accessed 24.09.19)

15   Sjoestedt (2000) p. 93

16   https://treesforlife.org.uk/into-the-forest/trees-plants-ani-mals/mammals/bear/ (accessed 24.09.10)

17   Green (1992) p. 53

18   O'Regan (2018) p. 236

19   O'Regan (2018) p. 236

20   Rolleston (1995) p. 121

21   Sjoestedt (2000) p.57

22   Sharkey (2013) p.42

23   Sharkey (2013) p.42

24   Carr-Gomm (1996) p.31

25   Carr-Gomm (1996) p.32, my emphasis.

26   Sjoestedt (2000) p. 93

27   Shepherd and Sanders (1985) p. xiv

28   Matthews (2017) pp. 1 -2

29   Matthews (2017) pp. 292-293

30   Matt Ward quoted in https://www.theguardian.com/uk-

news/2016/apr/24/kingly-statue-plunges-sword-into-tin-tagels-arthurian-row (accessed 27.09.19)

31 Monaghan (2014) p. 173
32 Jones (2017) p. 20.
33 Shepherd and Sanders (1985) p.125
34 Green (2011) p. 174
35 O'Regan (2018) pp.236-237
36 Sjoestedt (2000) p. 93
37 Rolleston (1995) p. 121
38 Sharkey (2013) p.42

Chapter 3

1 Shepherd and Sanders (1985) p. 1
2 Shepherd and Sanders (1985) p.59
3 Shepherd and Sanders (1985) p.60
4 Shepherd and Sanders (1985) p.60
5 Prósper (2018) p.121
6 http://theses.univ-lyon2.fr/documents/getpart.php?id
   =lyon2.2009.beck_n&part=159143
   (accessed 14.01.2020)
7 http://theses.univ-lyon2.fr/documents/getpart.php?
   id=lyon2.2009.beck_n&part=159143
   (accessed 14.01.2020)
8   https://www.timelessmyths.com/celtic/gallic.html/#Andart
   (accessed 15.01.20)
9 Monaghan (2014) p. 173
10 Monaghan (2014) p. 173
11 Monaghan (2014) p. 173
12 McKillop (2004) p.16
13 Monaghan (2014) p. 173
14 D'Este (2005) pp 10-11
15 https://www.britannica.com/topic/Artemis-Greek-goddess
   (accessed 16.01.2020)
16 Kaufmann-Heinimann, trans. Dr Eva Funk (2002) p.54.

17 D'Este (2005) p.20

18 D'Este (2005) p.21

19 Shepherd and Sanders (1985) p.62

20 Shepherd and Sanders (1985) P 62

21 https://www.bearfootwalkingtempleofursa.com/temple-of-ursa (accessed 17.01.2020)

22 Jones (2017) p. 68

23 https://www.skylightpublishing.com/gullylir/artha-about.htm (accessed 17.01.2020)

24 Jones (201) p. 69

25 https://otherworldlyoracle.com/bear-goddesses-bear-god-across-cultures/ (accessed 17.01.20)

26 https://otherworldlyoracle.com/bear-goddesses-bear-god-across-cultures/ (accessed 17.01.20)

27 Shepherd and Sanders (1985) p.xiv

28 https://www.druidry.org/library/animals/bear (accessed 17.01.2020)

29 Shepherd and Sanders (1985) p.136

30 https://www.druidry.org/library/animals/bear (accessed 17.01.2020)

31 Shepherd and Sanders (1985) p.59

32 Sjoestedt (2000) p.93

33 Hallowell (1926) p.162

34 Hallowell (1926) p.32

35 Hallowell (1926) p.44

36 Hallowell (1926) p.46

37 Hallowell (1926) p.59

38 Frazer (1993) p.264

39 Shepherd and Sanders (1985) p.110

40 https://www.quora.com/What-does-the-name-Beowulf-mean (accessed 28.01.2020)

41 https://www.britannica.com/topic/Beowulf (accessed 28.01.2020)

42 Shepherd and Sanders (1985) p.34

43 https://www.druidry.org/library/animals/bear (accessed 28.01.2020)

44 https://www.britannica.com/topic/Gwydion (accessed 28.01.2020)

45 https://mythopedia.com/celtic-mythology/gods/gwydion/ (accessed 28.01.2020)

46 Davies (ed) (2017) p.52

47 Davies (ed) (2017) p.48

48 De Bell. Gall., vi, 17 (tr Edwards) quoted in Sjoestedt (2000) p.20

49 https://mythopedia.com/celtic-mythology/gods/gwydion/ (accessed 29.01.2020)

50 Palmer (2001) p.36

51 Palmer (2001) p.35

52 Palmer (2001) p.35

53 Palmer (2001) p.35

54 www.sacred-texts.com/neu/kveng/kvrune46.htm (accessed 10.02.2020)

55 www.sacred-texts.com/neu/kveng/kvrune46.htm (accessed 10.02.2020)

56 www.sacred-texts.com/neu/kveng/kvrune46.htm (accessed 10.02.2020)

57 Shepherd and Sanders (1985) p.122

58 Shepherd and Sanders (1985) p.60

59 Shepherd and Sanders (1985) p.60

60 Shepherd and Sanders (1985) p,62

61 Shepherd and Sanders (1985) pp.63 -64

62 PGM VII, 686-690 accessed at https://archive.org/details/TheGreekMagicalPapyriInTranslation/page/n193/mode/2up (accessed 31.01.2020)

63 https://www.druidry.org/library/animals/bear (accessed 31.01.2020)

64 https://www.constellation-guide.com/constellation-list/bootes-constellation/ (accessed 31.01.2020)

65 Shepherd and Sanders (1985) pp.67
66 Shepherd and Sanders (1985) p.60
67 Sjoestedt (2000) p.93
68 De Bell. Gall., vi, 17 (tr Edwards) quoted in Sjoestedt (2000) p.20

Chapter 4

1 http://claras.me/2016/11/mary-plain/ (accessed 21.02.2020)
2 Rae in Bond (1971) p.75
3 Rae in Bond (1971) p.77
4 https://www.standard.co.uk/news/world/three-bear-cubs-dance-forest-finland-a4366601.html (accessed 21.02.2020)
5 Pullman (1998) p.180.
6 Pullman (1998) p.181
7 Pullman (1998) p.196
8 Sjoestedt (2000) p.93
9 Pullman (1998) p.190
10 Philip Pullman (2001) p.173
11 https://cahnrs.wsu.edu/blog/2016/07/grizzly-bears-use-tools/ (accessed 21.02.2020)
12 De Bell. Gall., vi, 17 (tr Edwards) Sjoestedt (2000) p.20
13 Pullman (1998) p317
14 http://www.old-engli.sh/dictionary.php (accessed 23/02/2020)
15 www.tolkiengateway.net/wiki/Beorn (accessed 23/02/2020)
16 Tolkien (2012) p.135
17 Tolkien (2012) p.135
18 Tolkien (2012) p.145
19 Tolkien (2012) p.153
20 Tolkien (2012) p.335
21 Tolkien (2012) p.335
22 Tolkien (2012) p.152
23 https://screenrant.com/pixars-brave-is-the-bear-and-the-bow/ (accessed 23/02/2020)

24 Shepherd and Sanders (1985) p.62
25 https://smite.gamepedia.com/Artio (accessed 28/02/2020)
26 https://www.youtube.com/watch?v=rnBNlnIevqA
    (accessed 28/02/2020)
27 https://www.youtube.com/watch?v=BpPxgm3ayaQ
    (accessed 28/02/2020)
28 https://www.gaystarnews.com/article/brief-history-gay-
    bears-scene/ (accessed 28/02/2020)
29 Les Wright, editor, *The Bear Book*, Third edition, Routledge,
    Abingdon, 2013, p 21

Bibliography

Batey, Colleen E., *Tintagel Castle*, English Heritage, London, 2010.

Bieder, Robert E., *Bear*, Reaktion Books, London, 2005.

Bond, Michael, *Michael Bond's Book of Bears*, Purnell, London, 1971.

Carr-Gomm, Philip and Stephanie, *The Druid Animal Oracle*, Connections Book Publishing Limited, London, 2005.

Carr-Gomm, Philip and Stephanie, *The Druid Animal Oracle*, Eddison Books, London, 1996, new edition 2019.

Cunliffe, Barry, *The Celts: A Very Short Introduction*, Oxford University Press, Oxford, 2003.

Davies, Sioned (ed), *The Mabinogion*, Oxford World's Classics, OUP, Oxford, 2017.

D'Este, Sorita, *Artemis*, Avalonia, London, 2005.

Frazer, Sir James, *The Golden Bough*, Wordsworth Edition Ltd, London, 1993, reprinted from 1890,

Gimbutas, Marija, *The Living Goddess*, University of California Press, London, 2001.

Green, Miranda, *Animals in Celtic Life and Myth*, Routledge, London, 1992.

Green, Miranda, *The Gods of the Celts*, The History Press, Stroud, 2011.

Hallowell, A. Irving, 'Bear Ceremonialism in the Northern Hemisphere' in *American Anthropologist*, Volume 28, No 1, January to March 1926.

Heaney, Seamus, *Beowulf* (Bilingual edition), Faber and Faber, London, 2007.

Jones, Kathy, *The Ancient British Goddess*, Ariadne Publications, Glastonbury, 2017.

Kaufmann-Heinimann, Annemarie, *Dea Artio, die Bärengöttin von Muri*, Glanzlichter aus dem Bernisschen Historischen

Museum 9, Bern, 2002. Translated by Dr Eva Funk for the author.

Matthews, John and Caitlin, *The Complete King Arthur*, Inner Traditions, Rochester (VR), 2017.

McKillop, James, *Oxford Dictionary of Celtic Mythology*, Oxford University Press, Oxford, 1998, reissued 2004.

Monaghan, Patricia, *Encyclopaedia of Goddesses and Heroines*, New World Library, Novato, 2014.

Müller, Felix, *Art of the Celts*, Thames and Hudson Ltd, London, 2009.

O'Regan, Hannah J., 'The presence of Brown Bears Urus Arctos in Holocene Britain: a review of the evidence', in *Mammal Review 48*, 2018.

Palmer, Jessica Dawn, *Animal Wisdom*, Thorsons, London, 2001.

Prósper, Blanca María, 'The Venetic Inscription from Monte Manicola and Three termini publici from Padua: A Reappraisal', in *Journal of Indo-European Studies* 46, Number 1 & 2, Spring/Summer 2018.

Pullman, Philip, *The Amber Spyglass*, London, Scholastic, London, 2001, reprinted from 2000.

Pullman, Philip, *Northern Lights*, Scholastic, London, 1998, reprinted from 1995.

Rae, Gwynedd, 'Mary Attends a Party' in *Michael Bond's Book of Bears*, Purnell, London, 1971.

Rolleston, T.W., *The Illustrated Guide to Celtic Mythology*, Studio Editions, London, 1995.

Shakespeare, William, *The Winter's Tale,* ed. Ernest Schanzer, Penguin Classics, London, 2015, first edition 1986.

Sharkey, *John, Celtic Mysteries*, Thames and Hudson, London, 2013

Shepherd, Paul and Barry Sanders, *The Sacred Paw*, Viking Penguin, New York, 1985.

Sjoestedt, Marie-Louise, *Celtic Gods and Heroes*, Dover Publications Inc, New York, 2000.

Tolkien, J.R.R, *The Hobbit*, Harper Collins, London 2012, reprinted from 1937.

Toynbee, J.M.C., *Animals in Roman Life and Art*, Pen and Sword Archaeology, Barnsley, 2013.

Vogler, Christopher, *The Writer's Journey*, Michael Wiese Productions, Studio City, 2007, reprinted from 1998.

Wright, Les (ed), *The Bear Book*, Third edition, Routledge, Abingdon, 2013.

Media Resources

The Battle of the Five Armies. Dir. Peter Jackson. Warner Home Video, 2014. DVD

Brave. Dir. Mark Andrews and Brenda Chapman. Walt Disney Home Entertainment, 2012. DVD

His Dark Materials. BBC, 2019. DVD

The Desolation of Smaug. Dir. Peter Jackson. Warner Home Video, 2013. DVD

The Golden Compass. Dir. Chris Weitz. Entertainment in Video, 2008. DVD

Online Resources

Arctolatry.org: www.arctolatry.org

Arthurian Knights Blog on Bear Gods: http://arthurianknightsride. blogspot.com/2009/04/artois-artus-arthur-bear-god.html

Arm the Bears article on Bear Goddesses: http://www. armthebears.com/home/2016/9/28/a-gift-for-you-artio-bear-goddess

Bear Tribe: www.beartribe.co.uk

Beth Wildwood, Etsy Shop: www.etsy.com/uk/shop/WildSpirit Weaver

Constellation Guide: www.constellation-guide.com

Coventry Telegraph: www.coventrytelegraph.net

Eifel National Park, Germany: www.eifel.info

Encyclopaedia Britannica: www.britannica.com

Evening Standard: www.standard.co.uk

Feminism and Religion, article on Artio: https://feminismandreligion.com/2015/08/26/artio-celtic-goddess-of-wild-life-transformation-and-abundance-by-judith-shaw/

Gay Star News: www.gaystarnews.com

Glastonbury Tor; That Strange Hill: www.glastonburytor.org.uk/mysterytor.html

Goddess School, article on Artio: http://goddessschool.com/projects/wavewalker/l1fpartio.html

Greek Magical Papyri available at Archive.Org: https://archive.org/details/TheGreekMagicalPapyriInTranslation/page/n193/mode/2up

The Guardian: www.theguardian.com

Hannah Willow: www.hannahwillow.com

Journal of Celtic Studies in Eastern Europe and Asia-Minor: https://balkancelts.wordpress.com/tag/armagh-bear-statues/

Journeying to the Goddess, article on Artio: https://journeyingtothegoddess.wordpress.com/2012/02/03/goddess-artio/

L'aróre Celtique: http://www.arbre-celtique.com/

The Kalevala, available at Sacred Texts: https://www.sacred-texts.com/neu/kveng/

Mythopedia: https://mythopedia.com

Neatorama: https://www.neatorama.com

Old Engli.sh: http://www.old-engli.sh/

The Order of Bards, Ovates and Druids (OBOD): www.druidry.org

Otherworldly Oracle: https://otherworldlyoracle.com/

Quora: www.quora.com

Revolvy: https://www.revolvy.com

Santuário Lunar article on Artio: www.santuariolunar.com.br/en/goddess-artio/

Screen Rant: https://screenrant.com

Smite, Artio Announcement: https://www.youtube.com/watch?

v=BpPxgm3ayaQ

Smite, Artio Reveal: https://www.youtube.com/watch?v=rn
BNlnIevqA

Smite Gamepedia: https://smite.gamepedia.com/Artio

Sunny Side Up: http://claras.me/

Temple of Ursa: www.bearfootwalkingtempleofursa.com

Timeless Myths, Celtic Deities: https://www.timelessmyths.
com/celtic/gallic.html

Tolkien Gateway: http://tolkiengateway.net/wiki/Main_Page

Trees for Life: https://treesforlife.org.uk

Université Lumiére Lyon 2: http://theses.univ-lyon2.fr/docu-
ments/getpart.php?id=lyon2.2009.beck_n&part=159143%20

University of Texas at Austin Website, article on Bears in Sami
Culture: https://www.laits.utexas.edu/sami/diehtu/siida/reli
gion/bear.htm

Warwickshire County Council: https://apps.warwickshire.gov.
uk

Washington State University: https://cahnrs.wsu.edu/blog

The Wheel of Britannia: www.skylightpublishing.com/gullylir/

Wild Place Project: www.wildplace.org.uk

**MOON
BOOKS**

PAGANISM & SHAMANISM

What is Paganism? A religion, a spirituality, an alternative belief
system, nature worship? You can find support for all these defini-
tions (and many more) in dictionaries, encyclopaedias, and text
books of religion, but subscribe to any one and the truth will evade
you. Above all Paganism is a creative pursuit, an encounter with
reality, an exploration of meaning and an expression of the soul.
Druids, Heathens, Wiccans and others, all contribute their insights
and literary riches to the Pagan tradition. Moon Books invites you
to begin or to deepen your own encounter, right here, right now.
If you have enjoyed this book, why not tell other readers by
posting a review on your preferred book site.

Recent bestsellers from Moon Books are:

Journey to the Dark Goddess
How to Return to Your Soul
Jane Meredith
Discover the powerful secrets of the Dark Goddess and
transform your depression, grief and pain into healing
and integration.
Paperback: 978-1-84694-677-6 ebook: 978-1-78099-223-5

Shamanic Reiki
Expanded Ways of Working with Universal Life Force Energy
Llyn Roberts, Robert Levy
Shamanism and Reiki are each powerful ways of healing; together,
their power multiplies. *Shamanic Reiki* introduces techniques to
help healers and Reiki practitioners tap ancient healing wisdom.
Paperback: 978-1-84694-037-8 ebook: 978-1-84694-650-9

Pagan Portals – The Awen Alone
Walking the Path of the Solitary Druid
Joanna van der Hoeven
An introductory guide for the solitary Druid, *The Awen Alone* will
accompany you as you explore, and seek out your own place
within the natural world.
Paperback: 978-1-78279-547-6 ebook: 978-1-78279-546-9

A Kitchen Witch's World of Magical Herbs & Plants
Rachel Patterson
A journey into the magical world of herbs and plants, filled with
magical uses, folklore, history and practical magic. By popular
writer, blogger and kitchen witch, Tansy Firedragon.
Paperback: 978-1-78279-621-3 ebook: 978-1-78279-620-6

Medicine for the Soul
The Complete Book of Shamanic Healing
Ross Heaven
All you will ever need to know about shamanic healing and how to become your own shaman...
Paperback: 978-1-78099-419-2 ebook: 978-1-78099-420-8

Shaman Pathways – The Druid Shaman
Exploring the Celtic Otherworld
Danu Forest
A practical guide to Celtic shamanism with exercises and techniques as well as traditional lore for exploring the Celtic Otherworld.
Paperback: 978-1-78099-615-8 ebook: 978-1-78099-616-5

Traditional Witchcraft for the Woods and Forests
A Witch's Guide to the Woodland with Guided Meditations and Pathworking
Mélusine Draco
A Witch's guide to walking alone in the woods, with guided meditations and pathworking.
Paperback: 978-1-84694-803-9 ebook: 978-1-84694-804-6

Naming the Goddess
Trevor Greenfield
Naming the Goddess is written by over eighty adherents and scholars of Goddess and Goddess Spirituality.
Paperback: 978-1-78279-476-9 ebook: 978-1-78279-475-2

Shapeshifting into Higher Consciousness
Heal and Transform Yourself and Our World with Ancient
Shamanic and Modern Methods
Llyn Roberts
Ancient and modern methods that you can use every day to
transform yourself and make a positive difference in the world.
Paperback: 978-1-84694-843-5 ebook: 978-1-84694-844-2

Readers of ebooks can buy or view any of these bestsellers by
clicking on the live link in the title. Most titles are published in
paperback and as an ebook. Paperbacks are available in traditional
bookshops. Both print and ebook formats are available online.

Find more titles and sign up to our readers' newsletter at
http://www.johnhuntpublishing.com/paganism
Follow us on Facebook at https://www.facebook.com/MoonBooks
and Twitter at https://twitter.com/MoonBooksJHP